CRUSADERS

CRUSADERS

The Radical Legacy of
Marian and Arthur Le Sueur

Meridel Le Sueur

with a new introduction
by the author

MINNESOTA HISTORICAL SOCIETY PRESS
St. Paul • 1984

*The photographs used in this book
are from the collection of the author.*

Minnesota Historical Society Press, St. Paul 55101

International Standard Book Number: 0-87351-174-3 Cloth
0-87351-178-6 Paper

Manufactured in the United States of America

10 9 8 7 6 5 4 3 2 1

Library of Congress Cataloging in Publication Data

Le Sueur, Meridel.
 Crusaders.

 Reprint. Originally published: New York : Blue Heron
Press, 1955.
 Includes index.
 1. Le Sueur, Arthur, 1867-1950. 2. Le Sueur, Marian,
1877-1954. 3. Socialists—United States—Biography.
I. Title.

HX84.A2L4   1984   335'.0092'2 [B]   84-14696

To my mother and father:

Valiant leaders in the people's struggle for peace,

freedom, and justice

CONTENTS

INTRODUCTION
TO THE REPRINT EDITION

For the convenience of the reader, a glossary of historical and social terms and names used herein will be found at the end of the book.

X

Crusaders,

This is the present that was the future Marian and Arthur Le Sueur spoke about in the wilderness that is now our past, a wilderness in which they shouted, like the prophets of old. They warned, exhorted, and taught so that their grandchildren and great-grandchildren would hear and be guided to the seventh generation. What they prophesied has come true, in even more disaster and suffering than they saw. When I see the world's refugees fleeing on all the roads of the earth, looking up in terror at the sky, and the children starving and the earth blasted, I not only think of Marian and Arthur, but I see that they also lived and fought under these same oppressions, against depressions, wars, terrorism, and hunger.

Marian fled with her three children from Texas in 1910 because there she was a slave, property of the father-husband, William Wharton. She fled north over the Texas border into Oklahoma where women had the vote in the early organization of the state. My father tried to extradite us, kidnap, invade, and possess us. In 1917 we fled from Fort Scott, Kansas, after the vigilantes had destroyed the People's College with ax and fire, took the back roads to escape the gangs that tarred and feathered and tortured all who opposed World War I. In the basement of our house on Dayton Avenue in St. Paul, we had a clinic to remove tar and feathers from objectors to the war. (You can die if too much of the skin is covered, and tar is almost impossible to remove.) Rocks were thrown through our windows and antiwar literature was burned on the front lawn.

We were often evicted from our homes. Men would come to the door at night knocking, wanting some of that "free love," and my Gramma in her nightgown would stand with a mop for defense and warn them how they would burn in hell if they touched a hair on our heads. The House Committee on Un-American Activities and F.B.I. stooges sat for two years outside our door watching us. Our phones were tapped. There was no way to make a living; terror was a daily emanation to us and our children. Marian and Arthur warned in their teaching that this was the action of a dying imperialism and it would grow worse and worldwide.

Their glory was that they wrote, taught, spoke, and pointed out the enemy. Their glory was that we lived a wonderful life and never knew it was a hardship or a martyrdom or a task. We belonged to a great multitude of men and women in the Midwest and the world who in fires of struggle commit themselves to a mighty contest. We were never alone. Some people say it was a hard way to live—I say it's the only way to live, committed to the people's struggle.

They both came from a long journey of migrating freedom fighters, from the Christian democratic church and the big revivals where thousands gathered, camping in tents with great orators and speaking tongues, and singing the birds out of the trees.

Marian's family were Christian democrats, abolitionists, defenders of the Indian. Her father was a brilliant lawyer on the Lincoln circuit in Illinois, probably a Hegelian anarchist. Her mother was the daughter of an Iroquois and an Irish rebel, who was also a friend of Robert Ingersoll and whose father was a big shot in the Presbyterian church; they were itinerant preachers also, a great and varied root.

In 1917 Marian married Arthur Le Sueur. His parents had rowed across the English Channel to the Isle of Jersey with Victor Hugo after the failure of a revolt against the French government in 1871 and rowed back at night with leaflets. They came to Minnesota and broke the potato market and followed the paths of the losers, the evicted, the mortgagors foreclosed by greedy bankers. Arthur took the seeds of his radicalism from two events: he watched his father horsewhip the banker who had taken their land, and he later revolted against Bishop Henry Whipple and religion by calling upon God from the middle of a field to strike him dead if he was up there. Arthur went on plowing, an agnostic the rest of his life. He never lost that compass, pointing to the predator, the enemy.

These people were like many pioneer crops, a great and wild root, vital travelers, through dark conceptions, wild migrations, like the wheat came to the prairie, multiplying like the people in a new and rich and deep soil, divergent seed, conduits of light and bread, and high vision of new crops. Traveling over continents they came for freedom, for the continuation of the new and shining human, bursting from inherited seed, herbal protein, all repeating and burgeoning into an abundance never before known on earth. The abundance is multiplied in genetic expectation. The abundance jetting from the seed, brought in sunbonnets and pockets from the Old Country, carbon from the air, oxygen making sugar, the raw materials of work and love—nitrate, potash, the leaf clasps the stem pits, the blade clasps, the culm, grains enclose the bride encased. David Fife, a Scottish immigrant to Canada, planted five grains of a new kind of wheat from one stalk. Two were eaten by oxen, three produced other stalks each with five grains. Next year there was a bushel of wheat. In four years there were 500 bushels from one grain, in ten years 2.3 million bushels. In 1916 we grew enough wheat to feed 500 million people.

Arthur and Marian have more than thirty grandchildren and great-grandchildren.

Converging, luminous, alive, we emerge out of the ancient seed. Converging, migrating in love and solidarity.

I was born to my mother in 1900 when she was captive of her early marriage to a Protestant minister of the Disciples of Christ, captive of a patriarchal world in which she had no rights, not even of having her own soul. She married my father as she graduated from Drake University in Iowa where she could not take mathematics or science— only domestic arts and languages! She could not own property, and my father could collect her wages if she had a job. You cannot understand her courage, to leave him, to go north like a black slave woman, with three children and having never earned her living. In the night she kidnaped us into Oklahoma, a new state with many socialists, where women voted in school elections and had almost gained universal suffrage when the oligarchy took over. We fled to my grandmother's house in Perry, Oklahoma, where we were the minority, the Indians having just been robbed of their land and government. Marian, a shy woman, became a speaker in the Chautauqua circuit, a remarkable cultural phenomenon where thousands of people came to a huge tent that acted as stage for the only outside culture they had. She spoke on Love and Bread, attacking the slavery of women who could not have love when what they needed was bread. An old yellow clipping quotes her as speaking for a nine-hour work day for women and on the forcing of women into prostitution because of their scandalously low wages. She spoke for the freedom of women over their own bodies and the right not to have children they cannot feed. The penalty for giving any information on abortion or contraception was ninety-nine years in prison. She was tried in Kansas City, Missouri, for giving birth-control information to a woman with fourteen children. The woman refused to identify Marian and was given three years in prison. She left her fourteen children under Marian's care.

Women in Arkansas and Missouri and Kansas flocked to Marian after her lectures, begging for some birth-control knowledge. She was a magnificent presence (as all the yellowed newspaper notices testify) and brilliant and also very beautiful.

We lived in Perry in a little white house my Gramma had built after she went on the 1889 Oklahoma run for Indian land in a horse and single buggy with a whip and a gun. She got this land and with an old carpenter got river stone for the foundation, and built this cottage which is still in good condition and now lived in by Indians.

I left high school in my freshman year, and I never went back. They did not teach my history or the account of the struggles of my people. That tremendous time before World War I has not been documented, a dangerous wiping out and darkness of the true history of the people. There was the reality of the democratic struggle going on around me. In 1900 Jim Hill and Pierpont Morgan agreed to combine the Great Northern and the Northern Pacific railways, despite the Populist laws against cartels. The manipulation and exploitation roused the farmers to form the Non-Partisan League in North Dakota which for one year, 1919, governed the state, building a mill and a bank, taking over the coal fields to protect the striking miners. The Populist party which included the South, labor, and Negroes proclaimed—

> The party of the common people, the child is come and it is a giant at birth. The blood circulates in a million hearts which from the depths cry out for a better life. Its sledge hammer swings with the muscles of the toiling army, its songs will come out of the oppressed, the thrones of despotism are trembling. The rights of man rise triumphant and decree that the poor shall no longer be the inheritors of toil, nor wealth the reward of man's knavery. To your tents O Israel. Build your prairie fire where the flames will cast lurid lights in the glassless windows of your sod Shanties. Be ready! Be nervy! Be strong!

I got my education at these great picnics, meetings of farmers, lumberjacks, miners, factory workers. They came for miles, some hiking, some in long lines with great banners—"We ask for justice." "We want land." It was a pentecostal of politics. Speakers went up and down the countryside. Arthur traveled all over the Dakotas with the huge map he unrolled in schoolhouses, ringing the bell and telling how the wheat exchange by the stroke of a pencil was robbing them of millions. Everyone was talking, learning, listening. Farmers, mechanics, ranchers, hoboes, wanderers, itinerant workers mounted soapboxes, shouted in wheat fields, passed out leaflets at factory gates. And gaunt sun-tanned women who had rarely spoken now rose at meetings, and there were singers, and everyone could write his own piece and pass it out or pile it on the tables at the meetings. Tongues of flame, witnesses to the agony of the farm evictions. All were touched with prophecy and utterance.

The landscape changed, the plow had a new meaning, objects became alive in the hands of the people who were not going to be silent. They rose and spoke as the oppressed and objectified their exploiter. Most of all they discovered the fire and wonder of solidarity.

It was not only a theory, an abstraction—it was a physical arousal. I went with Arthur to the Mesabi Range during the iron miners' strike and saw pregnant women taking over the picket lines when the men were arrested. The fat local priest with a crucifix hanging between his knees brought all the threats of hell, enjoining them to leave, shaming them, and they threw rocks at him and he fled. I went into their shanties and saw men who couldn't breathe, lungs turned to stone from silicosis. I wrote about them. I could never forget them.

I saw the Finnish poet who never rode but walked the Mesabi, working and saying his poems in Finnish. These men are going to rise, he cried, rise in the eyes of themselves, in the eyes of society. The day is dawning.

In Oklahoma they had the moonlight schools where, after harvest, the whole family camped out. There were classes in economics, socialism, history, and there was dancing to the fiddle and accordian, and home theater with skits and poetry and original song and home-grown comics. And the children had special education in mutual aid that taught them how it was better to lift a rock together and maybe understand leverage and learn to build a machine. It was a counter-culture of collectivity instead of dog-eat-dog. It was antimonopoly and antiwar.

In that period before World War I there was a great movement of the democratic and radical forces. There was immense activity in the labor movement. Thousands joined unions during strikes in Paterson, New Jersey, and on the iron ranges of Minnesota—strikes led by the I.W.W., who organized the wheat workers and on the West Coast the marine workers. The Red Special in 1908 carrying Eugene V. Debs and also Arthur Le Sueur toured the country, pausing at whistle-stops and in the wheat fields with crowds lining the tracks. Mass socialist activity reached a high point in the 1912 elections and also in 1918 with the strong antiwar sentiment that has never been documented. There were national daily and weekly socialist papers exceeding two million circulation in 1913. There were also trade and union papers, and foreign-language socialist dailies and weeklies in addition to cultural and theoretical magazines. There was the *International Socialist Review* that was circulated worldwide. The *Appeal to Reason*, edited in Girard, Kansas, had eight hundred thousand subscribers and could in a week circulate a special edition of a million copies, as it did on the Mexican revolution. There were also about twelve hundred Populists and Socialists elected to office in municipalities, including seventy-nine mayors, one of whom was Arthur, mayor of Minot, North Dakota, from 1912 to 1916. The antiwar movement was greater than has ever been estimated. At the 1917 Socialist convention, the midwestern faction led by Marian and Arthur Le Sueur split with the East, voting against the war and struggling to carry out the opposition. Debs was imprisoned and ran for president from jail. He got over a million votes. When one remembers that this was a time of the disenfranchisement of the black people and that women could not vote, this is astonishing.

We dared not go to a movie or even to church and were jeered at and even spit upon on the street. We were driven out of Fort Scott after the college had been sacked, papers destroyed, and we fled to St. Paul, where the Non-Partisan League still had an office. Charles Lindbergh, Sr., voted against the war in Congress and was himself almost tarred and feathered at a peace parade in Red Wing. They threw red paint on the cars and Lindbergh crossed a pasture to get away from the mob. A train was coming down the track with a Non-Partisan League engineer who picked up Lindbergh just as the mob bore down upon him.

One of the great experiences of my life, changing me forever, was the Ludlow massacre. The story of the organization of the Western Federation of Miners is one of the great sagas of the West. The miners north of Trinidad, Colorado, went on strike against the Rockefeller mines in 1913. They were evicted from their homes and had been living in a tent colony below the mines near Ludlow. They had dug cellars under their tents to be out of the weather and out of the gunsights of the Rockefeller militia that shot from the hills. One night in 1914 the militia shot into the pits below the tents and set fire to the colony, killing the women and children and one of the miners' giant Greek leaders, Louis Tikas, filling him full of gunshot. He was buried in Trinidad at a great mass ceremony to which the great labor organizer Mother Jones had been secretly smuggled to speak. Farmers and workers had started toward Ludlow with their rabbit guns. The mines were surrounded by the army. Now the miners, the fathers of the dead children, and their martyred wives came to Fort Scott to raise money for their support. They were starving. They were blacklisted. They had lost the strike. They moved over America being seen and their wounds were bound by comrades. They marched down the street of Fort Scott silently, their bodies bent from the mines as if the sky also rested on them. They were gaunt sorrowing men. They were Armenian and Greek with the faces of Jesus. The faculty of the People's College marched behind them. I held my mother's hand. We were weeping. And some of the people on the sidewalks wept also and ran out to clutch their hands or embrace them. Others stood meanly and stolidly and silently as we passed. I saw the bodies bearing the mark of their oppression, of their stolen labor, and now their holy dead. Their bodies were hieroglyphs of their exploitation, their blood and bodies taken, their lungs turned to silica stone, a strange sadness and even humiliation in them but also something else, a terrible fire and grief.

When the march ended on the lawn of the People's College, they all broke and embraced and wept. They showed pictures of their children alive and pictures of them dead, still looking surprised to be killed in their sleep. They had pictures of Tikas with forty slugs in him as he tried to protect the children. And I'll never forget that evening in the workers' hall where we all sang and danced. There was something between us that could never die and now I recognize it in the world happening now, in the global identity with suffering and struggle.

They drew in some of the Kansas roundheads, old puritans who weren't used to dancing with men, and then they drew the women blushing and crying into the great circle, and the frail floor shook but held.

This reality was powerful, rousing the true image of our condition, moving from silence of the victim and of old structures and guilt, the fatal dormancy of establishment education which made the condition seem destined, unchangeable, god-given. We saw the enemy. We saw that our failure was not our own, that we were not the mob, inferior and ignorant, that we were not doomed to adapt to the depression every four years where you lost everything, to unemployment and perpetual wars against people whom we did not know.

The People's College, founded in 1914 by Debs, Helen Keller, Charles P. Steinmetz, a local radical named Shepherd, and Marian and Arthur Le Sueur, in Fort Scott, Kansas, was not only a Socialist college. It initiated the most radical methods of opposing the banker system of education as they called it, beginning a method of teaching workers and farmers how to think collectively and see the hidden reality in their own condition, originating their own response to oppression. This method is now becoming worldwide in the teaching of Paola Friere of Brazil who is introducing his theory of the Pedagogy of the Oppressed in new democratic countries. He believes language is a tool of oppression, teaching humility, docility, fate, and the belief that nothing can change. He believes there should be no teacher and student, no authority but a system of dialogue in which the true reality will emerge. Especially he points out the corruption when the word and the action become split. All reality must be based on the word and action bearing upon absolute change. The oppressed should not learn the language of the oppressor.

The new teachers looked for books to use at the college, but it was clear none of the standard books was adequate. So they had to write their own books and curriculum that would say: "I work, and working I transform the world." They had to have a curriculum that would make evident the viable reality, the responsibility of the democratic people to recognize the real world, to name it, to regain their humanism which had been stolen from them.

Marian edited the *People's News*, a weekly that was sent to the students of the correspondence courses in workers' law, workers' English, history, bookkeeping, elocution, journalism. She wrote, urging them to take these courses. "What would you do," the ad said, "if you suddenly woke up to find power had been thrust upon you? Do you feel that you would be prepared to play your part in initiating and aiding the work of a new society? Let us help you to organize your knowledge— can you write a good letter? Can you talk clearly, spell, convince the other fellow? A whole year's course, five cents a day, fifteen minutes a day. Study economics, workers' history, woman suffrage, eugenics, and natural sciences. Dialogue cannot take place between antagonists. You must learn from those who have the same problems and need the same solutions."

She wrote a course that was published in 1917 as a book on workers' English. (In an essay I wrote for a university, I said this and the editor noted on the side, "There is no such thing.") The book was called *Plain English, for the Education of the Workers by the Workers.* Debs thought it was a milestone in workers' consciousness. The book said the sentence was like solidarity among the workers, five fingers that made a fist. All the examples were from democratic and revolutionary literature. The farmers began to write asking where they could get the rest of the quotations. So my mother suggested to the Appeal to Reason Press in Girard, a short trip south, that they print what became known as the Little Blue Books, to fit in the overall pocket, sell for a nickel, and contain excerpts from Jefferson, Lincoln, and Tom Paine, and later poetry and jokes and satire. You could carry them anywhere, whip them out while riding a freight or resting from plowing in the wheat fields.

It was in Fort Scott that I also got my education. It was a radiant center, not only for the Midwest but for travelers who came through from all over the world. Alexander Berkman, the anarchist, a dark, Semitic, elegant man with a mustache and a cane, startled the natives by appearing soon after he was out of prison. Some mothers ran out and grabbed their children as he passed, fearing the devilish presence of an anarchist. My grandmother left the house during his stay with us. Since my mother went to work at eight o'clock, I gave him breakfast, and he would talk to me like an equal human being, telling me about the steel strike at Homestead, how the Pinkertons came up the river and shot into the town, and how the workers defended the town with even the mayor on the picket line and the great hearths shut down, and how he, a young man, felt he should point out the evils of the Carnegie power by shooting its manager, Henry Clay Frick, for which he served sixteen years in prison, mostly in solitary. He did not succeed in killing Frick. Then he told me about the impressionist and cubist painters, a changing art, from illustration to so-called realism, and about writers like Theodore Dreiser and Frank Norris and Jack London, who were showing the reality of American life. He said the greatest most holy thing was to be a writer of the revolutionary people, to give your life and never betray them. I was thirteen.

The workers came from the Oklahoma oil fields, young men with huge arms, storytellers, and some died at the college from injuries at work and from hunger. They had stories to tell of wandering, of long hours of work and low pay, of separation from their families left behind in the Ozarks. Lean farmers, poor as the land they tilled, came like bodies driven to the utmost, some came walking to find this glowing center. One Arkansas hillbilly began to dance when he got the idea of surplus value, that it was not the boss who charitably gave him a job, but that he was the creator of wealth and it was stolen from him. I saw grief. I saw sorrow. I saw the psychic death that came from feeling you are a failure, among the despised and dispossessed. I saw them become human beings with each other. The landscape changed for me. I was never again struck alone or swamped with private sorrow, never a lone person. I knew we must be human again.

We had big parades on May Day and Labor Day, and the I.W.W. would come down from Kansas City where they often had schools and centers of education. Some of the townspeople would be peeking out of windows, standing alone. Then there were picnics and dancing and lectures at the school. The college executive committee met at the college at least once a year, Keller and Steinmetz and Debs kissing everyone. Kissing was not part of the culture of the Midwest or of the puritan. My grandmother never kissed anyone over two years old. But Debs kissed you truly, as a comrade, a human being, and an honored fighter. There was a tradition that four girls all in white should each present Debs with one red rose. We walked up out of the audience and Debs, tall, lean, and bent over like a worker, would cup our faces and kiss us tenderly with a cosmic salute to our struggle, and we would stumble off amid the great applause. Debs also embraced men, holding them as valiant allies, thumping them on the back, re-embracing them. Arthur thought this was excessive. He thought Debs was very emotional, but he loved him.

It seemed to me Arthur expressed his folk feeling and affection by telling about his boyhood, about defending innocent drifters and members of the I.W.W. and the trials of hundreds who were against the war. He boasted that not one of his I.W.W. clients went to jail. He had a great prejudice against making a trial into a propaganda stage in which, as he said, you polarized the judge so he had no choice. He had several disagreements over this issue with the radical movement, withdrew from cases that turned the defendants into mouthpieces of the movement. He was very adamant, saying that his role was to free them, not to use them as propaganda. Many clients did not agree with him, seeing their arrest as a forum to publicize their cause.

On the other hand, he was a master propagandist. In his files are three-page, single-spaced letters to every new president after each election, telling him what the needs of the people were. He and Marian and a group of farmers wrote their own draft for the Treaty of Versailles. In his files is an impressive detailed legal document on how to form the League of Nations and preserve peace for all our inheritors. There are also letters to editors, letters to leaders about to cave in, betray the cause, letters of hearty support when they stood tall against the giants of power.

Woodrow Wilson refused to let the farmers go to Versailles, refused them a passport, and told them to go home and not meddle in "that of which you know nothing." That strange phrase, "in that of which," so stiffly grammatical, stuck in Arthur's craw. No Le Sueur got a passport for forty years.

The People's College was literally destroyed by the war, with fire and ax, as was the Non-Partisan League. The jails were full of conscientious objectors and I.W.W.s and Minnesota had an officially sanctioned vigilante committee, the Commission of Public Safety, headed by the governor, that was like a fascist junta.

Our counter-culture, the underground collective, held even when the Non-Partisan League was destroyed. From its ashes, phoenix-like, rose the Progressive party of Wisconsin and the Farmer-Labor party of Minnesota. Both grew underground during the war, appearing in the twenties and growing until the depression when the Farmer-Labor party elected Floyd B. Olson as governor. They were a part of the reality of the New Deal which changed America and led to the C.I.O. It was from the roots of this frontier democratic prairie fire that we all kept alive and grew into the global history now firing the earth. They never lost faith or expectancy or belief.

The war was a disaster. It was the bloody amalgamation of world capital. I was eighteen. Hardly a boy of my class or time returned from Europe. I considered it the grave of my generation. I wanted to die. Those who did return were gassed, sick, embittered. The poets, the fathers, the seers of my generation were killed.

The long struggle to break away from Europe was deepened in the Midwest. My grandmother would not read a book from England or listen to Beethoven. She remembered her Irish father telling of singing "Give me a grain of corn, mother" as they came to America to escape starvation. Although she never spoke of it, her Indian mother must have borne a terrible bitterness, brought to Illinois to a white puritan village that never accepted her.

The reaction set in after the war, and there were many suicides. The trade unions were smashed. In 1919 there were the Palmer raids, in which in one night thousands of Socialists and Communists were arrested, jailed by the order of U.S. Attorney General A. Mitchell Palmer. Arthur defended hundreds of people in Minnesota alone. The Progressive party was killed. And below what was laughingly called the "Jazz Age" showed the terrible face of the prowling beast . . . the depression.

We all came together at 2521 Harriet Avenue in Minneapolis which became a historical place. Some people still remember the telephone number. My two brothers and their wives, me and my two children, and Marian and Arthur all were sailing the muddy waters of the depression in this small, wooden, floating, rocking, two-story house. It was a place to put your misery together. Arthur somehow maintained his office in Minneapolis. (After his death, many old men came up to Marian and promised to pay back what he had loaned them during the depression.) He told his stories. He had stories I later saw in old newspapers, including a wonderful one about a farm woman who hid her lover in the wood box. When her husband returned she finally smuggled him out in a bearskin. A hilarious story. And at home he had his Hoppergrass stories for the children—a shame there were no tape recorders then. Sometimes we had to walk to town barefoot to save shoes and carfare. My brothers' wives had low-paying jobs, the rent was thirty-five dollars, and Marian was a genius in making cheap and nourishing dishes. She was proud of "making do" with the money we scrounged. When the first free food was offered, before the New Deal, white flour and powdered eggs, she was too proud to claim it. My brother and I went down and brought it home. White flour was anathema to her, and nobody knew what to do with powdered eggs.

They had prophesied the depression. They had taught society's weakness and its inevitable path to unemployment, disaster, complete breakdown. This had happened according to their scientific analysis, so this was a time of bringing in the crop, which is most ripe when the system fails and our true condition is revealed in naked suffering and visibility. Our poverty was the common condition, and our revolt became necessary. The hunger marches started. The great people's organizations, the Workers' Alliance and the unemployed councils, sprang up out of the marsh and Arthur was their witness, their defender. Marian spoke to the Farmer-Labor clubs that were growing on the despair and ruin of the farmers. The cities were alive with meetings, protests, hunger marches—emaciated men marching down Nicollet Avenue behind a sign, "We live on Minneapolis relief." At the first great demonstration outside the city hall, thousands of hungry people massed for blocks and the mayor refused to see them. But the city fathers made a mistake and threw tear gas bombs out the city hall windows, and some of our baseball players caught them and pitched them right back. They exploded inside and those bureaucrats ran out, holding their noses, and the committee met with them right there on the steps, all crying and negotiating food for the hungry.

As the depression deepened there were meetings on Harriet Avenue and committees, plans, conversations, feeding of hungry people, farmers bringing in apples and rutabagas and pig jowls and beans. In the morning Marian and I would come downstairs and see the people rolled up on the floor sleeping. We would peek in to see who it was. Do you know this one? Looks like that Workers' Alliance fellow from Milwaukee. Once it was Pete Seeger on his way hitchhiking to Duluth to collect songs of timber workers and steelworkers. Once it was Woody Guthrie. The house was marked, as many were in the country, with all the wanderers collecting where there was organization or trouble. Stories were told of the plan in Chicago to fight the evictions by having groups move the furniture back into the houses as it was put out on the sidewalks. Stories were told of hundreds of people sleeping under bridges in the parks. There were things to write about. Added to everything else there was a terrible drought. I went to North Dakota to report it for the *New Republic* and as I slept on the grass of a farmer's place, the grasshoppers ate off my left pant leg.

The silence was broken now. The people were talking. I went to penny sales where people bid a nickel or a penny for a farm and the women took off the pants of the auctioneer and locked him in the barn and left him. It was plain now how the National Association of Manufacturers had kept Minneapolis a company town, defeated all attempts at unionization. The average wage had been twelve dollars a week for a twelve- and fourteen-hour day and a six-day week.

Such a time is a wonderful coming alive of the people. We were like farmers who had planted, and now got a rich crop, a rich and powerful flow of the reality they had prophesied and promised. The illusion had shattered, the magician was revealed as a trickster, and the sight and release of this realization and anger of the people was a joy to them. In 1933 as Franklin D. Roosevelt won the presidency, the Farmer-Labor party elected Floyd B. Olson as governor and a friend sat in the Capitol, an old I.W.W., a wheat-field worker.

They were part of government. To be a radical was almost a necessity for getting a job. The whole city changed. In 1934 Olson appointed Marian to the State Board of Education and to the State

Planning Board. Arthur was appointed municipal judge by Governor Elmer Benson in 1936. The Truckers' Strike in 1934 broke the back of low wages, made Minneapolis a union city. I was on the Federal Writers' Project, Marian and Arthur were teaching and speaking again with a recognition in their community. Arthur was attorney for the Teachers' Union and for the newly organized C.I.O., battling again on the range.

The C.I.O. sent me to the Mesabi Range to expose the danger of silicosis, which was suspected of being a killer. But there was no recognition of it, and no range doctor would diagnose a single death as death from silicosis. I had not been there a day when I received calls to stop my investigation and get off the range—or else. Years later, when veterans came to the veterans' hospital in the Twin Cities to die, it was diagnosed and was eventually made compensible.

The struggles did not stop, as they never do. Marian and Arthur had no illusions about the dynamics of power. Reaction took over the state again with a terrible anticommunist, anti-Semitic attack. We went swiftly to World War II and all that followed: the terrible Holocaust, the millions dead, under the hooves of conquerors. The earth was full of the slain, but the flesh opened in resurrection in the dark, to the end of the war, and the dropping of the bomb. My mother and I sat in a darkened room in sorrow and grief. She said this is the beginning of a world struggle. Now they have gone too far. They are ready to kill us all. They must be stopped.

If they made a miscalculation, those great rebels of our past, it was the inability to imagine the final brutality of power. They could not see the logical instrument developed that would kill the earth and its people. They did not warn us of the final brutality: that if the powerful decide that the bomb will let them preserve their power, they cannot save themselves or even remain human. But neither could the rebels envision the global power of the oppressed that the bomb would unite, the oppressed who would become the gravediggers of the predators.

But I cannot criticize their heroic warning and their faithful love. It becomes like a turning lighthouse beacon throwing directions to us, maps we never thought of, new social structures of peace and abundance, images of a new reality. How clearly they saw that and showed it on their maps in country schoolhouses and spoke of it from soap boxes on city streets, always threatened by arrest. What they said and did now appears strong and amazing, moving in new directions, in the enormous battles of the dispossessed to regain and protect our humanity.

Their lives become more amazing, like negatives kept in a chemical. The true picture gradually emerges, astonishingly clear and beautiful.

Unlike elitists and intellectuals, they never gave up hope, never were addicted to cynicism, disbelief, or philosophical defense of what they called failure. They never failed. The consciousness of the people was always raised by any struggle. The enemy is always there, growing larger, and the suffering becomes unbearable and the image is becoming litmus-clear as the giant becomes more naked, more brutal, more visible.

In these difficult and harsh circumstances we have to perceive, as they did, the dialectics of this struggle, to keep what Blake calls the "divine wisdom." In the poison, the acid rain, the nuclear threat, we see the cries of the new birth, the heroism of anonymous guerilla workers of every color and nation, their human faces and bodies beckoning us, calling, mouthing words out of silence.

The Indians say each generation is responsible to seven generations for their root in the earth, for their spirit in the nation. The shapers and the givers believe that there are those who will go before and come after in a great human weave, calling and responding, remembering, awakening. We look forward to them with love and expectation, not greed and possession.

We live by our vigorous likeness and love and the remembering heart, so we speak to the embryo, "Be not afraid," and the new children come out beautiful and free. We move toward each other in our own light, move toward each other in exalted reciprocity, human shepherds and lovers in constant flesh and lighted desire.

They illuminate their children and grandchildren and the children of the earth.

They have come this way. We have awakened together.

We shall come this way perpetually. We shall come this way with the children of the earth. Wake us to flame and tide.

You see their insistence of life, continuity, that whatever is done has resonance with all.

They never lost hope or expectancy of the new, or their faith in the human, in the heart of the people, the only herbal cure and balm. Their belief is now made visible. What they prophesied is happening even beyond their luminous faith. From a small planting, one grain of wheat, producing, justly and logically, grows enough bread to feed the world. They showed us the patience and the planting, the seeding and the awaiting and the nourishment, the heat and the nitrogen, the formed image out of the terrestrial flesh, green life again out of the living bones, freedom appearing in the crop that never runs out, the path of the broken and massacred, rising in generous giving and proclamation for living, not death. They seized it from their ancestors and we seize it from them for the children. The loving tilting of the earth shows us your moving toward us on loving horizons, and you come fully forth out of our own pain, redeeming humanity from all holocaust.

You gave us life.

We promise the continuation of life.

In all children. In all love.

Meridel Le Sueur

CRUSADERS

"There is a wall of which the stones
Are lies and bribes and dead men's bones.
And wrongfully this evil wall
Denies what all men made for all,
And shamelessly this wall surrounds
Our homestead and our native grounds.
But I will gather and I will ride,
And I will summon a countryside,
And many a man shall hear my halloa
Who never had thought the horn to follow;
And many a man shall ride with me
Who never had thought on earth to see
High Justice in her armoury."

Hillaire Belloc.

I

ARTHUR LE SUEUR, 1867-1950   MARIAN LE SUEUR, 1877-1954

This is a short history and evocation of the lives of
Marian and Arthur Le Sueur. Born in the years shortly after the
Civil War, they plowed a deep furrow in the nineteenth and
twentieth centuries. Arthur Le Sueur was born two years after
the end of the Civil War, and five years after Lincoln's signing
at last, of the Homestead Act. That Act brought floods of migrations from the old countries, where, since the failure of the
'48 revolutions, workers and farmers had pressed against the
crowded ports, seeking to get passage to the new lands where
bonanzas were promised and it was said the birds flew, fried a
golden brown, into your mouth and the streets were paved with

gold. They came from the Jersey Isles where they fled in rowboats from Normandy, after the rise of Napoleon and the crushing of the people's struggle in France in 1794. Their house had been a refuge for the exiles of '48, including Victor Hugo who sat with the children on his knee, imbuing them with a staunch hatred for the rising bourgeoisie and the colonialism of Britain and France.

Marian Le Sueur was born ten years later, of a line of English remittance men and Irish rebels and the Dutch and Indian marriages they made crossing the Wilderness Road on the Lincoln trail, some stopping at Toulon, Illinois and others following the opening of land into Iowa, Texas and Oklahoma. She was of the mid-west village life, the democratic square, courthouse, small farm, town hall; the revolt of women; the agrarian reform movements; the picture of Ingersoll on the coffins of the dead.

To understand both them and ourselves, the times that begot them must be understood; the struggles of their nation, and every form of struggle the people waged against the usurpation of power, for the guarantees of the Constitution and the Bill of Rights in the period of the beginning of the growth of monopoly, expansion and gigantic cartelism. Their greatness lay, as it does in all of us, in the extent that they partook of the destiny and fulfillment of the experience of their nation, fought against its mutilation, embodied in flesh and blood all the agonies, all the lessons, even the fearful errors, all the struggles to conquer reality, all the triumphs and despair of our people across three generations of history.

In their youth the depression of 1873 gave them their

first and deep lesson in the growth of industrialism controlled by growing cartels: amalgamation of gigantic robbers, which would lead to wars of colonial seizures, two major world wars, and the atomic bomb.

To understand their great strength and their errors, their triumphs and the fierce grip they have on our future, which we cherish, not only in memory but in action, in affection, in tensions and in strengths, we must review the long period through which they lived. There were two forces mounting to world conflict that we and our children must resolve in the future: on the one hand, the powerful growth of state and world imperialism; on the other, the growth of the American people's movements; and, affecting my parents deeply in their later days, the great rising of over half the colonial peoples of the earth.

We must look at our inheritance as both memory and the future, rushing back, demanding action.

My people did not leave me land, or wealth, or great empires. I have on my desk a small inheritance, an instrument to estimate the prairie curve which my grandfather used, carrying out the plan of Thomas Jefferson, who saw a patterned, mathematical future in America, nothing hit or miss with a tree or a fence mark; but a survey clear as the Bill of Rights, set to the light of Polaris, of Aldebaran, of the Big Dipper, true to the moon and the sun and the needs of men, ignoring all that eroded, moved, changed like ridges and rivers. This was part of the democratic accuracy and justice.

The mapless, formless wilderness, alive in the subtle mind

of Dakota, Pottowatamie, Fox or Chippewa, was henceforth marked clearly in orderly titles in the severe democratic court houses. Each township of six miles square was divided into thirty-six sections, each one mile divided into four equal quarters, each full section measuring six hundred and forty acres, including the road, with errors in curvature and measurement caused by the earth. Each quarter was the historic one hundred and sixty acres, the free homestead, the dream of every starving, hounded worker on the docks of Dunkirk. My grandfather carried this instrument through the dark nights waiting for the sight of the stars to set the meridian.

Now I have always cried to these forebears and cried to them for answers, for compasses, and seen their deeds, their actions, solid and muscular. They have always put a marker up at the place of disaster, guided your hand to the fissure of the mortgage and the quitclaim; pointed out the assassin, identified the murderer, the usurer, the depraved. They have kept records of the Long Trail of Tears, the Battle of Wounded Knee and how many were killed by government bad beef; kept the bone splinter and the shoes of the dead child. Now, in a moment of crisis and cold, they point out where the warm ash of the old fires can give you warmth, where strength is cached. I can even catch their heraldic voices in the wind of struggle.

My family came from all the great migrations. They came on the stinking boats after the famine of '48; the black Irish, following the farms west. The migration is the common experience of us all, of both my red and white fathers and mothers. The Trail of Tears, still alive with migrations—the migration from seized tribal and ancient and deeded lands into raw dust and alien corn—is known to us all. Where I lived in Kansas it was said that ninety thousand went through there on the way to the Oregon Trail. They also trailed back. My grandmother sat in her buggy on the line of the Indian Territory of Oklahoma, when the stolen land was opened as a state. With her shotgun over her knees, she made the run and held the land till the claim was filed.

They wore the country on each foot. They salted it with their sweat, changed it with their labor, and had little more than six feet for their bodies. They kept alive the dignity of dissent and the right to impose upon it change; the cry for justice.

They were dissenters from England, Campbellites who could no longer stand the feudal property relations of the Church. They were circuit riders in Kentucky and educators at Oberlin, the first college in America to grant degrees to women. They manned underground stations before the Civil War.

They saw the steady impoverishment of land and people. Marian's family lost the rich farm lands her grandfather had helped to survey. Arthur's family broke the Chicago potato market, lost the rich land at Nininger, and homesteaded again in Dakota. His father went on to the mines hoping to strike it rich but died instead of tuberculosis.

As young people they saw their depressions, their wars, and the deepening of class war. In the 1890's great strikes involving thousands of workers hit back at the National Association of Manufacturers, which represented the new cartels. The Pinkertons, like the present F. B. I., organized violence and espionage against the workers, the destruction of civil liberties and the attack against the foreign-born.

It was the period of asking why for the petty bourgeois radical, the small business man and the farmer and intellectual, alike menaced by this rising power. It was the time of the panacea, of utopia, of the speaker at the small meeting, the church, the picnic, the opera house jammed for the anti-monopoly debate; of the tour over the farm country with the co-op chart, the Socialist books for sale, agrarian radical newspapers—the *Appeal to Reason,* and also the *Iconoclast,* edited by Arthur Le Sueur when he was Socialist mayor of Minot, North Dakota.

The Village and farm agnostic was very verbal, for he had to break away from fear and the terror of Calvinism and its hellfire. It was the season of money panaceas and cranks. Anyone with a reform or solution for monopoly printed and distributed his idea or spoke from any prominence. It was a time of great creativeness of the people, of the development of wheat, of the blacksmiths' wrestling with the problems of the plow and the harrow and the great reaper. But alas, the people did not reap anything but disaster from this great bonanza.

It must be clearly known, and was stated by my parents: there is only one force that creates value and that is labor, and one manner of expropriation of wealth, the exploitation of labor and the natural resources. Empires were built by the seizures of Indian lands—nineteen million acres in Minnesota, three million in Iowa and as many from the Pottowatamies of the Illini—and by the seizure of timber, and timber land, in more millions of acres, much of it sugared off, stolen or given outright. Speculators and railroads grabbed one-eighth of Illinois, Wisconsin, Iowa and Missouri and Minnesota, and one-third of Arkansas under the "Swamp Land Grants" in 1849. Farmers who later bought back this land paid fifty million dollars for it, and then lost it again to the mortgage holders who accumulated millions of unearned wealth, in what the Populists called "the multiplication of nothing."

In Minnesota alone, in a deed of night, the Territorial Government gave the Northwest Railroad land grants which covered an area larger than four eastern states. A new group of thieves, the Minneapolis Millers, sprang up on the wheat bonanzas. Organized in three centers of power, the Chicago Board of Trade, the Duluth Board and the Minneapolis Chamber of Commerce, they catapulted great fortunes with only the stroke of a pencil. They made millions in the mixing house alone, selling themselves the same bushel of grain and giving themselves a commission for the robbery. There was dockage for dirt, false balances, and phantom switching costs, and there were hives of commission men, speculators and elevator managers.

The farmer driving madly from one elevator to another found they were all controlled by the same bosses, whose sway extended to every spur of railroad, excluding all competition or freedom to market. He found that the banks were also owned by them, that he was ruled by powers he could not see and hawked on world futures without his say. A man he could not see, on Fourth Street in Minneapolis, pressed his finger on the telegraphic key and dictated what price should be paid for wheat in every town, and there were no other buyers.

"There has been enough money stolen from the farmers by the wheat ring," said Ignatius Donnelly, candidate of the Populists, "to pave the road to hell with gold."

This great steal and great lie pointed to resistance by the people. Marian and Arthur Le Sueur were part of these movements—Arthur of the United Socialist Party of 1901, the I.W.W., the Socialist Party under Eugene V. Debs, the Non-Partisan League, and the Farmer-Labor Party.

The outlaws have lived so long upon the surrounding country that they believe it to be their inalienable right to live upon it. Amazing is the testimony brought out by the investigation and exposure of the millers. They maintained their actions were not immoral or predatory. They morally sanctioned stealing on the grounds that everybody did it and it was their unchallengeable right. They had the audacity to cover their rapacity by the assumption that any critic of their thievery must be a "foreign agent" or a "dangerous red."

We can now estimate the land poverty and erosion but we find it more difficult to estimate the human erosion, to make a map of deprivations, of the mad women at screen doors, of the Joads with the sadness of all immigrants, the small farmer on the road again.

But there has been a further erosion, the erosion of memory, of purpose, of accurate charts for the journey. These charts of a trail and a direction made by such fighters as Marian and Arthur Le Sueur make a path for us all. They make it easier to down the fear and the slowness; they make more sturdy those who remain silent, or are tempted by the rewards of the lackey, the informer, or just the "collaborator." They make the path to the future so bright and indestructible that the death bed confessors, the criers of return to old shelters, to dead ideas, to feudal fathers, are put to shame.

It is true that old Socialists truly never die. They never fell into sloughs of depression, cynicism, unbelief, or despair or inactivity. An easterner said to my mother in 1952, "It's a terrible thing, all the failure of the third party movement, such energy, gone to waste, lost. . . ." My mother, then seventy-five years old, was running for Senator on the peace platform of the Progressive Party of Minnesota! They sense no failure of any kind, knowing the future is secured. They have faith in these strengths continuing.

Agrarian Socialists from the beginning of the century, with skill and agility they participated and led in the struggles of the people; they arrived at the foremost post, but not too far ahead. They sensed, like compass needles, the direction of all struggles against monopoly; the need for agrarian reform, the breaking of power in the cities by organized labor, the alliance of every third party and reform movement of the worker and farmer. While regional leaders, they were internationalists of a passionate kind, excited by every atttempt of man to break the fetters of body and mind.

Socialism was their culture, action, poetry, life itself. Social good was their only good. They contributed stintlessly

11

to the education of our people. Arthur Le Sueur, with his map, went to every village, every county in the Dakotas to get out a leaflet, ring the school bell, set up the map, and show the face of the predators! They went by hand car, horse, and model T, and they met in pastures when they were banned from speaking in the villages. When he was the Socialist mayor of Minot, his first act was to order the balls and chains of county prisoners thrown into the river. He was sued for this by the Republican City Council!

Stones were thrown through our windows during World War I, yellow paint thrown on our car. In the rural court house where they practiced law together, the Le Sueurs defended the foreign born, the men and women arrested for opposing the war, the Socialists, the Non-Partisan Leaguers who were tarred and feathered. Wherever there was a fight they were there. They seemed to have something we sometimes lack, a terrible, wonderful lust for the fight.

Arthur returned like Ulysses from every fight and told how he bested the prostitute judges, how he stood against the Vigilante committees, how he bested them in argument. When he was dying at eighty-three, he was still fighting. In his delirium he made preparations for civil rights struggles, and he hoped to live to see the freeing of Korea. The thousand veins of his social passion rose out of the corruption of the body. He did not want to see the minister they asked to send him—said he would stand by the facts until it was out of the realm of "speculation". He died in the year of the Smith Act. He wanted to defend us all and, in delirium, worried by the fact

12

that he had no "wealth" to leave us for our defense, he conveyed schemes to us of ways of fighting.

My mother in the same way, her children and grandchildren hounded by the F. B. I., her phone tapped, had visions of the "singing tomorrows"—and wished only to stave off decay long enough to see that great future with our people singing in peace on the great prairies.

They left a compass greater than my grandfather's. They left their names in the great smoking texts of the peoples' struggles, to be read as volcanic and water movement on rock or glacial terrain. They lived upon the storm, were refreshed by disaster, cut their teeth upon loss, walked out like David for the fight, laughed at the puny merchants with jaundiced eye on profit, broke all indictments and injunctions against thought, or assemblage, asked for amnesty from all verdicts of madmen and assassins, shook the prairies with gigantic laughter at the corporations' laws against majority or minority thought. They knew that the people, like the giant pines, rise up from below and two-thirds of the strength and nourishment is below ground. They always walked out upon these unseen strengths and always partook of them. Inquiries and litigations they ignored, or went to court armed with thunderbolts of insolence and contempt for the puny servility of newt-eyed judges, lickspittles of monopoly. On their death beds they planned further forays, defenses, attacks, hazardous and gay, the enterprise of all revolt, knowing the great works of the people, composing all the time.

In the slow, brave, tortuous movement of the agrarian struggle, they were moving toward Marxism, aware that sharper instruments must be had for the stronger struggles. Slowly, in analysis, they saw their instruments had been failing; they saw the viciousness, the vastness of the enemy, the failures of reform, the inadequacies, as Arthur said, of electing "the fox to look after the hen coop."

Their bitter struggles had bitter lessons; they saw the great wave of the future rise and fall back into silence and seeming sleep. They looked and saw the new weapons in China. They left reluctant, sensing great battles, eager to be in them.

Their compass points toward the inevitable weapon of Marxism. Their strength continues in us at the portal where they always stood, the door to the future. Our faces bare to the bone, our mouths gagged with the wind, we walk in deeper paths than they knew. They had a dream, we *see* the reality. Even our enemies are weaker than theirs, for capitalism is a decayed, faceless nightmare, exposed by the people of the world, who reach across the world market to touch hands, to affirm again relationship and love.

This is our inheritance.

"Ill fares the land, to hastening ills a prey,
Where wealth accumulates, and men decay."
                                        Oliver Goldsmith

"Oh for a man who is a man, and as my neighbor says, has a bone in his back which you cannot put your hand through."
                                        Thoreau

II

ARTHUR LE SUEUR, 1867-1950

Arthur Le Sueur was born December 7, 1867 in Nininger, Minnesota of Amy and John Le Sueur, recently come from the Jersey Isle with all their kit and kaboodle. Amy had her embroidery, her harp, and French gold-leaf embossed songbooks; John his tools, jewels, and enough cousins to work the new Homestead land. They built a mansion not far from Ignatius Donnelly's and shared the hopes of the inhabitants that Nininger would become the river port and the greatest metropolis on the upper Mississipi. But through some skulduggery, the Hastings across the river and St. Paul up the river got the port franchise, and a one-eyed robber baron named Jim Hill got a franchise for a defunct railroad in St. Paul. John Le Sueur raised so many potatoes that he broke the Chicago potato market and had to dump the potatoes in the Mississippi river caves, a lesson in supply and demand which Arthur always said has some relation to a bald-headed man with abundant whiskers. He was born nine years after the founding of the state and the scandalous railroad bond swindle, two years after the Civil War and the assassination of Lincoln, and six years before the terrible depression of 1873. From his mother he breathed the air of Voltaire and the rights of man, and even the name of Mary Wollstonecraft. His father was an authoritarian Episcopalian, a man full of temper and stubborness, but gentled by the life of Amy Le Sueur who kept up the linen tablecloths, the paintings and songs, and the big fires of an evening. But when her sixth child was born she was thrown from a farm wagon and lost the child and died herself.

Arthur was around five then. Unable to pay the banker, they lost the big mansion and had to move into poorer quarters. All the boys had to plow and hoe and John Le Sueur became a bitter and stern man. They did their own cooking, usually oatmeal and molasses, and Arthur did not gain his growth till he was nineteen. After that he grew three inches.

The boy at eight plowed the sand of the river bottoms and had much to think about. He was learning lessons of bankers, property, marriage and religion, and deepening those strains of contemplation and poetry, always strangely emerging from the frontier man with the stern Normandy face, peculiarly like the Indian faces of the Dakotas.

He wrote these things down many years later. These are his own telling:

"Looking back I can see how my mother tolerated my father's fanaticism rather than believed in it. She was a woman, played the harp in the roustabout river town, sat at her needlework, did hand illuminated copies of French roundalays. She told of long talks with Victor Hugo. After her death my father probably lonely, with his brood of motherless children and constantly failing, he began to punish us severely as he had never done when mother lived. He became silent and then violent and fanatical. I was very seriously inclined to get to heaven where my mother was. I suffered the terrors of the night and the eye of God which penetrated your every thought; and my father's eye in the early morning prayers and evening prayers as he looked at every one of us, examining our inmost secret thoughts, watching our actions, assuming everything was evil. I went to bed with the covers over my head praying to join my mother.

"He preached to us as the ax bit into the stump, as the plow turned the soil. His doctrine was that every word of the Bible was true. He believed in hell fire and the only salvation from sin, the sacrifice of Jesus. You couldn't get salvation unless you believed as he did and if you didn't have salvation you would go to hell. He would have had to invent a hell in any case to have a proper place to consign democrats and catholics.

"I was about eleven when we were walking side by side, coming back from work, and as usual, when swinging an ax or doing any work he was talking his religion and I cannot recall what he was proving to me but he said, 'We know that this is true because Christ said it was.' I said, 'Well, wasn't that true before Christ said it was, if it was true?' He hauled off with a right hand and slapped me with all his might, hitting me on the side of the head, knocking me tizzle and upwards. He usually used a leather strap with a buckle on it but this time he couldn't wait. Before I could get on my feet and my senses together he was shouting the doctrine down at me.

"But a boy like a man, convinced against his will, is of the

17

same opinion still. But this drove me to work out my own philosophy.

"The following summer I was plowing the field. I always thought of what Bishop Whipple would say when he sat in our front room. That room, never opened, was opened to him. Before my mother died I sat often on his knee and listened as he told about the Indians, what wonderful people they were. He did not look upon them as beasts as the others did. He even blamed the white treaty makers and told how he had appealed to Lincoln for amnesty for them. I remembered this all my life.

"Another influence, a happening that influenced me . . . My father had spent a fortune on his land on the river, and we had taken out a mortgage of ten thousand dollars with a Hastings banker who had a son who wanted to marry my sister Anne; but she did not care for him, so my father refused the money lender savagely and the money lender foreclosed the mortgage and one day we were hoeing our rented land which bore on the highway. My father so religious that he would not allow a fiddle or a pack of cards in the house.

"One day we were planting potatoes near this highway with a couple of neighbor boys and my oldest brother when the money lender and his son, driving a pair of spanking horses, drove by and my father, following his feeling of Christian duty that he must raise hell with everybody he disagreed with, stepped out on the road and hailed him and commenced to abuse him in polite terms. The money lender was afraid my father would snatch him out of the buggy so he lay whip to his lively horses and was away down the road to Hastings. But when he later returned he waited till we came back to the end of the row and shouted over the fence to us, 'I would like to know who could blacken the character of a blackguard like you.' My father swung his wooden country hoe with the heavy length of handle over his shoulder and went through a gap in the fence shouting, 'I will show you.' I followed behind to the fence and stopped when I saw the money lender and his son each had a revolver in his hand and the son shouted to my father who was advancing steadily, 'If you make another step this way I will shoot.'

"My father's civic as well as Christian ire was roused and he was sprinting toward the buggy, straight into the revolvers, and they both fired, but he kept right on going. They both jumped out of the buggy and the horse jumped away and my father jumped faster toward them, a thin spry man.

"They both took another shot at him and he kept coming and when he got to a hoe handle's length of the old man he brought his handle length down on the old man's head. Only the beaver hat saved his life. Then in the same gesture, he raised it again and I can see the picture to this instant, the young man with the big silver revolver in both hands, up to his eye, taking good aim and firing straight into my father's belly. But my father brought the hoe down on the young man's shoulders and he did not fire again but turned and ran.

"My Dad, a real sprinter, even with those bullets in him, chased the young man a quarter of a mile, then came back to us stunned, the blood sloshing out of his shoes.

"The shot had just missed his heart and he carried bullets in his back to his grave but he lived to sue the money lender and he kept his hoe in a convenient place conforming to his usual maxim, 'Trust in God but keep your powder dry.'

"But what influenced me the rest of my life was the trial which followed at Hastings with a lawyer named John Brisbane. I was a witness and as I came back I passed the counsel table and Brisbane reached out and got me by the arm and drew me close and patted me on the head and said, 'My boy, you will be a great lawyer someday.'

"For years after that, while on the river drives, working on farms and in the woods, when I tried to get the education and was the laughing stock at Ann Arbor where I was called the 'Bull of the Woods,' for twenty years, earning money in summers in the log drive until I finally passed the bar and set up my one law book on a kitchen table, I heard those words in that Hastings court house.

"The following summer I was plowing. We had left Nininger and gotten free land twenty-five miles west of Grand Forks on the Turtle River. It was late and cold and I had no mittens. I was plowing a walking plow with my bare hands and I felt an awful misery. Not only to endure the work of a man, and the oatmeal and molasses but the insult we had to endure in the way of preaching and condemnations on the sinfulness of boys and the certainty of hell for them.

"So I stood in the middle of the circle of sky and I asked out loud how did the old man *know* this was the truth? Who wrote the Bible? How did the men who wrote the Bible know it more than anyone else, and if I myself had no capacity for knowing all of it was that a sound basis for being condemned forever to hell?

"I cried the old cry—Strike me dead God and show me you are there!

"But there was the old silence. The plow and the cold and the earth were there. I went on in my misery from and to, furrow and back again. Suddenly it seemed to me there was only one way I personally could know anything of either God, man or creation. Impressions would come to my mind that I could rely upon, and be informed of these impulses through sight, hearing, smell, taste or feeling. Information was carried to my mind from God, earth and man, and no other way. All these impressions that got into my mind would be subject to adjustment one with the other and required calculation. There was no other way to figure out God and have an opinion based on facts.

"There had to be judgment, taking into consideration all the knowable facts about each item which the mind stored away. I had to learn all the psalms and the prophets so I began to find things to support my views. The heavens declare the glory of God; and the firmament showest his handiwork. Day unto day uttereth speech and Night unto night showest knowledge. So I saw the universe was big and I need not worry about going to hell, or a Being looking at me with hate.

"And so the sapling grew."

It is hard to follow the next years. In 1880 my father left the farm and hired out for eight dollars a month cutting cord wood and splitting logs. He became a logger in the winter and a thresher in the summer. He carried his books with him and studied. He had to figure out the words himself and always afterward pronounced them the way he first saw them. He saved his money to go to law school.

Around the fires of the lumber camp and in the heat of the harvest day he must have heard the high and low talk of the Haymarket struggle for the eight hour day, the depression of the eighties, the formation of the great agrarian organizations: the Grange, the anti-Monopolist Party headed by his old neighbor Donnelly, and the Farmers Alliance and the Populist Party; and talk of the organizations of workers in the Knights of Labor and the American Federation of Labor. He must have heard of the Pullman strike, the miners' strike led by Bill Haywood, and Coxey's army of the unemployed that moved on Washington. It was a period of great labor and farmer struggles, and he was among the men who had begun to get some political savvy. He certainly felt on his own back and knew in his blood the lash of the growing, ruthless exploitation, erosion and destruction. He saw men die under the great trees and cursed the endless wandering, womanless life of the "bindle stiff." By hanging on to his money, he was able to buy himself a threshing rig by the time he was nineteen. It was an old thresher, and he invented the first automatic tier for it. He saved enough from the summer's harvest to go to Ann Arbor to law school.

Here he was called the Bull of the Woods, in his lumberjack clothes. He studied so hard that he could see a whole page of Blackstone law and then recite it verbatim. He learned poetry at night and pleasured himself with his Dakota talent for story-telling and jokes.

Back in Fargo he went into the law office of a liberal North Dakota lawyer, Tracy Bangs, whom he loved all his life.

Later, he finally set up his kitchen table and one law book in the frontier town of Minot which lay between the cattle country and the wheat country. Men passed through there, going back and forth, following the crops and the westering cattle. Here the immigrants were settling. They came in box cars and in buck boards, the Russian Dakars, Scandinavians, Norwegians, Hungarians, Croatians. They needed lawyers and an honest one was a rarity. They came to the stocky, stubborn Bull of the Woods, Arthur Le Sueur. He began to be a lawyer.

This was in 1900.

There are marks of his struggle. There were choices to be made. A young lawyer could amass a fortune by dealing in titles. One of the first clients to come into Arthur's office was an emissary of the Empire builder, Jim Hill. He took cases for Jim Hill and then he took cases of the workers against Jim Hill. He became assistant to the Attorney General.

He seemed to have steered a windy course. He made money in investments, got a taste of the great barbecue, saw he could become a rich and powerful man. He also saw the poor immigrant rooked out of his land; he saw the men who had come to plow the land, build homes and raise families, pushed out by the railroad kingdom.

He watched the Socialist Party growing in this period. Founded in 1892, it polled thirty thousand votes in the year of the Pullman strike. In 1905 he attended the Socialist convention in Chicago. In 1908 he was on the Red Special of the Debs and Hanford campaign, and in 1912 he was socialist Mayor of Minot.

In this period he seemed to move steadily in the direction of the peoples' struggle which he was to follow all his life. He became a Socialist.

At that time an ideological struggle was forming the American working class. The Socialist party, as the leading party of the working class at that time, had many factions, rifts, splits, reformings. Arthur Le Sueur has in his files the tracks and trails of those struggles as they formed him, as he struggled within the class pressures of his place and time. Out of the roots of the agrarian movement, of grangers and greenbackers, from the European left wing of Marx and Engels, and the Bernsteinism of Germany and syndicalism of France, the Socialist Party made its struggle. It was made up of immigrants, poor farmers, and petty bourgeois radicals, doctors, lawyers, preachers and even priests. Its weakness was its isolation from mass organizations of labor.

Daniel De Leon had led the party with a strong authoritarian hand. Morris Hillquit led the faction against him and with Victor Berger and Debs broke away from the extreme left wing and helped unite a disintegrating party, with only independent state units and small groups of Christian Socialists, into a united Socialist movement. Their program was to "conquer the powers of government and use them for the purpose of transforming the present system of private ownership of the means of production and distribution into collective ownership by the entire people."

There were direct actionists, who later split off into the I.W.W. There were those like De Leon who wanted to fight only for Socialism and had no immediate demands, and there were trade unionists who wanted to fight for immediate aims and low key socialism. They all hated the A.F. of L. and most of them were dual unionists. They had right, left and middle. Their program was to fight for hours and wages, social insurance, equal civil and political rights for men and women, for the initiative, referendum and recall.

Arthur Le Sueur debated De Leon at Cooper Union on the money question. He argued with the left wingers on direct action and sabotage. He has files of letters of these theoretical discussions and criticisms. He began to travel and lecture and debate these questions. Papers, leaflets, pamphlets and books

24

were distributed, sold. The Socialist youth was organized, a magazine for women was edited in Chicago. Lecturers came into the territory and spoke at the picnics. Farmers carried in one pocket the *Iconoclast* or the *Agnostic* and in the other the *Christian Socialist*.

Along with the growth of monopoly, this period also represented the growth of the people in political and economic struggles, and the painful acceptance by the labor movement of theoretical knowledge and the necessity of education for the American working class. It was the time of the minds forging, of the sighing in the balance of the vaunted democracy. It was the time of the great gathering on the prairie, of the picnic with the Socialist speakers and the argument in the bunk house of the right and left of political and economic power, of the fronts to fight on and ways to do it, of how the worker and farmer might secure his land and the machine he operated, to get back at least some of the products of his labor. It was the time of the heated argument in the school house, of the speaker at the rear of the wagon who talked against the wind, against the cries of babies who, he warned, would be killed in the first world war. They rang the school bell, passed out leaflets, hung maps on the wall, and then got in their old Ford with the Socialist Party signs on it to go to the next meeting. They were refused halls and schools and churches, so they spoke in the open field, or in a barn, or in the big kitchens.

By 1912 the Socialist Party was at its peak, leading strikes, free speech fights, civil rights causes, political struggles. There were fifty-six Socialist mayors in five states; Emil Seidel was

25

elected mayor of Milwaukee, and Arthur Le Sueur mayor of Minot, North Dakota. There were one thousand and thirty-nine dues-paying members in elected offices. Debs and Seidel ran on the Presidential ticket and polled eight hundred and ninety-seven thousand votes. There was a strong Socialist press, with three hundred and twenty-five periodicals. The *Appeal to Reason* had five hundred thousand subscribers and got out large special editions that ran into the millions. Arthur Le Sueur edited his paper, the *Iconoclast,* in Minot which, in a crisis, could circularize the town and countryside in two hours.

Woodrow Wilson cried out that we were, on the verge of a revolution. The N.A.M. got behind Teddy Roosevelt to back reforms, and even started a third party to siphon off the militant protests.

There was also a struggle within the Socialist Party. Bill Haywood and others left in protest against the petty bourgeois character of the Party, dominated by millionaire socialists and professional and middle class members who fought against militant action, and moved toward collaboration with the corrupt A.F. of L. and Gompers. The Socialist Party never recovered from this split of its militant workers, and the outbreak of the war deepened the chasm. In the St. Louis convention one part supported the war and the left wing opposed it; many were tried and jailed, to emerge after the Russian Revolution and the debacle of the war to form the Communist Party.

Many leaders of the left, like Haywood, joined the I.W.W. Arthur Le Sueur seems here to have taken a middle road within the Socialist and reform movements, which he maintained with painful integrity all his days. He supported the I.W.W. while at the same time urging them to moderation. He was against the first World War, but believed that head-on collision against conscription was suicidal. He did not foresee the revolution in Russia and its effects upon the war and the world. He held on to his deep respect for Blackstonian law, believing it to be a great advance of the people in court. In this belief he often found himself at variance with many of his colleagues and often broke with the labor movement, but as always, he stuck to his belief and fought all comers for it. At the end of his life, blind and poor and virtually alone, he walked into court rooms where the attorney and the judge had already met and decided the case. But he still stood on the glories of the Chartist movement and the English law.

The *Iconoclast* of 1912 has the following item:

"Art Le Sueur is the apostle and high priest of Socialism in North Dakota. He was met at the station with the band and they marched to the Opera House . . . he spoke at the picnic and those that came to find that Socialism was a menace went away declaring it to be the hope of the world. Comrade Art is a forceful speaker. He puts up his charts and they receive close attention. Physically he is a strong man and impresses one with his sincerity and earnestness. When he gets through you cannot find a trace of where there was a Democrat in the township. . . . Also had a red hot ball game at the picnic . . . potato race and dancing . . . fifty-five books were sold. This is our year . . . we will be free . . . the mortgage is always with us. He drew up a wagon in a company town and made a speech and a little old man grabbed his hand. I been waitin' fer ye mister ain't had nothin' to vote for but Republican and Democrat and that's like choosing between a hog and a pig—since the Populist Party. I been waitin' twelve year fer ye."

Arthur Le Sueur at this time was also a banker. This reflects more than anything the contradictions and turmoil of the times. As a banker he acted in this way: The banks wanted to foreclose on cattle loans in the fall but they did not want to claim the cattle till spring. They did not want to extend the loans, but they wanted the farmer to feed the cattle all winter on range and then foreclose in the spring. Arthur Le Sueur sent out word to the Socialist farmers to come into town on a certain day. Over fifty came and he told them to line up at the bank and ask for an extension of their loan. When it was refused, they should all say the same thing: "Very well, come and get your property." When the bank said they could not get the cattle in the winter, the farmers were to reply: "Very well, then, I will bring my cattle into town today and leave them at the back of the bank!" The farmers lined up clear down the block. The bankers were frantic. The loans were extended!

In the summer of 1913 two I.W.W.s, Jack Law and Allen, came to Minot to organize the construction workers and teamsters. The business men came to Le Sueur to help them run the organizers out of town. A big construction job was going up and a union and a strike would lose them much money. The lawyer called their attention to the fact that the organizers had as much right in the city as he or any other man, and he warned them he would prosecute anyone who attempted, or incited others, to tar and feather them, or ride them out on a rail, or any criminal acts against the street speakers. For eight nights the organizers spoke peacefully and there was nothing but order. But Minot was a gamblers' wide open frontier town. It was run by power companies, the railroad, the wheat ring and the Commercial club working through thugs, piggers, and gamblers.

The evening of the ninth day the meeting was being held when a cigar manufacturer and a well known gambler drove a big car into the crowd and roared the muffler. Law, the speaker, kept order and adjourned the meeting. The next day seventy-five special police, thugs and gamblers were sworn in by the sheriff whose brother was the biggest gambler in the town. That evening a case of eggs was thrown from the top of a building into the crowd. Law and Allen held the people in check. The sheriff did nothing. On Sunday the tension was taut between the working class and the business men. A big crowd was milling around as the speaking started and the police began to pull the speakers down from the soap box. Then after twenty I.W.W.s had been arrested, the Socialists began to take the box and they were pulled down and arrested until over a hundred had been arrested. Then the mayor, Arthur Le Sueur, took the box. The police hesitated. "Arrest me also," he said. And they did.

Some of the men were brutally beaten. They stood in the cells, man to man, solid, and the hot water steam was turned on them. They tried to find informers but no one would talk or allow themselves to be bailed out, including the mayor. Many middle class Socialists, merchants, dentists and others, were in those cells. From the block Le Sueur conducted the defense. The *Iconoclast* reports the trial:

"Over a long protracted trial he brought out the proofs, made the issues clear. . . . 'If these men are guilty of the charges against them then I am decidedly so. Don't acquit me unless you acquit all the rest. Yours truly is more guilty than any of the others!' With these words he hurled defiance in the face of the representatives of the rotten and demoralized city fathers. Those blockheads sitting as jurors heard for the first time a discussion of the science of political economy. Comrade Le Sueur told them that the present organization of society makes the law serve the robber barons, and how the man owning the tools of industry becomes the master of the man using them."

Men and women had been driven from the city, habeas corpus was refused, men were convicted without evidence, men had been injured for life. The governor wired the mayor, accusing him of not keeping the peace, and Le Sueur answered:

"There has been no violence except that perpetrated by the police officers. I am for law and order all the time but I believe it as binding on the chief of police as any tramp. . . . I hold no brief for the I.W.W. and have no more sympathy for them than for any organization of working men and women! The officials in power have no respect for law and order, clubbing citizens, punching women in the ribs . . . if it is not stopped, you will be morally responsible . . . for here there is only the question of guaranteeing those few simple rights of personal liberty and security without which any government is nothing but a legal hell."

When at last the half-starved, beaten men were released they had no place to go, so the Socialists opened a camp and protected it with their own armed guards. The chief of police, despite the promise of the court, said to the mayor: "We are going to go out and get those S.O.Bs." Le Sueur told him: "They are sick from your lousy jails and they have to rest up. If you touch one hair of their heads I'll blow your brains out; I'll shoot you at sight. I'll blast your frail heads off." The police didn't go out to the camp.

They knew the gangsters would try to destroy the *Iconoclast* which put out a daily edition during the trouble. Two big I.W.W. cow hands, seven feet tall, stood outside the press door with all the deer and rabbit rifles they could muster in a heap beside them. When the sheriff and his boys came, the two said, "Just stay where you are on the sidewalk, boys." The Sheriff said, "You know it's illegal to be armed." "We're not armed," the boys said. "You can search us; those guns are just lying there but don't come any further, just stand there and we'll stand here and everything will be all right, but step over that step and you might be dead and you wouldn't want to be dead, would you sheriff?" So the Sheriff and his boys dribbled away.

There were five hundred armed Socialists waiting for the violence the Chamber of Commerce had prepared. Some of the bankers, lawyers, wheat kings and railroad barons left the state.

This was only one of the struggles. They introduced liquor control, slum clearance, they ran Arthur Le Sueur for the Senate. Arthur proposed at the I.W.W. convention that they unite with the farmers instead of fighting them; that they work only for farmers with a "red card," the I.W.W. member-

31

ship card, and thus control the labor market *with* the progressive farmer.

The I.W.W. established a long line of militant itinerant workers in the wheat and orchards from Oklahoma to Alberta.

Then the first world war broke.

Arthur left the state and went to Fort Scott, Kansas to head the law department of the new Socialist Correspondence School, the People's College headed by Debs.

Here he met Marian Wharton, come a long way to be a Socialist and head the English department at the new college.

Here they were married.

"He believed that happiness was the only good; reason the only torch; justice the only worship; humanity the only religion; and love the only priest.

"He added to the sum of human joy, and were everyone for whom he did some loving service to bring a blossom to his grave he would sleep tonight beneath a wilderness of flowers."

Robert G. Ingersoll

"My first American ancestor, gentlemen, was an Indian— an early Indian. Your ancestors skinned him alive, and I am an orphan. Later ancestors of mine were the Quakers William Robinson, Marmaduke Stevenson, *et al.* Your tribe chased them out of the country for their religion's sake.

"Roger Williams was an ancestor of mine . . . your people . . . burned him. . . . All those Salem witches were ancestors of mine! Your people made it tropical for them. . . . The first slave brought into New England out of Africa by your progenitors was an ancestor of mine—for I am of a mixed breed, an infinitely shaded and exquisite Mongrel."

Mark Twain

"With a great sum obtained I this freedom."

Aristotle

"Freedom's a hard bought thing."

Stephen Vincent Benet

III

MARIAN LE SUEUR, 1877—1954

After many migrations of her family, Mayme Lucy was born in Bedford, Iowa in 1877, where her mother Antoinette

McGovern Lucy had fled in the depression to her last farm. Her brilliant lawyer husband fled home whenever the bitter advent of another unwanted child turned her into an enemy. She had worked as a cook at Drake University, up to the last. She always had her children alone and later her husband would come back, start his brilliant law career again, and become the spokesman for what she called "the underdog," and a well-known criminal lawyer. He believed that the Civil War marked the end of American democracy; offers of judgeship, political plums, bought and paid for Senators, fat eaters at the barbecue table, all disgusted him.

He was a friend of Robert Ingersoll's and invited him for dinner; his wife allowed this in return for his refraining from practical jokes on her Campbellite ministers and missionaries from India. Her father had also been a dissenter, and carried a shilleleigh during the Civil War because he was outspoken in his belief that the war meant centralization of government, the development of corporate steals and the end of democratic jurisprudence and education. He taught at Oberlin where he had helped organize the underground railroad. In his own way he seceded from his country at the end, becoming deaf so as not to hear of it and dead with his devoted wife, who being of good health, died eight hours after he did. They were both buried in the field of the Toulon farm, and now, still in the field, a great granite stone keeps the plow in a tide around them.

The strong democratic men felt the defeat of the law and education, of the beloved principles and practices of Jeffersonian democracy, of the Christian Socialists; they saw the defeat of the land, the wars and depression. The families broke up, as the fabric of the land, the lost villages shook, scattered, broke in a toll of dispersion, disappearance, death, drunkenness, amnesia, and silence. "Where he went I do not know. He disappeared in the gold rush . . . at sea . . . Lord knows where." A card in the horse hair trunk saying "I am fine hope you are the same. . . ."

The women were often left alone, the men gone to better fields. The pattern of the migrating, lost, silent, drunk father is a mid-west pattern, and accompanying that picture is the upright fanatical prohibitionist mother, bread earner, strong woman, isolated and alone. My grandmother raised her own children, my mother hers, and I mine.

So upright in her beliefs, my grandmother carried on the upright puritan village life without ever knowing that the fight for the eight hour day impinged upon her, that the growing labor movement and struggle for wages, or the wars of annexation, had something to do with the fact that she lost her land, was often poor, and saw the old Scotch and Irish pushed out of their land by the new immigrants whom she came to hate. Searching for a cause, she laid it all to drink and became the Secretary of the Oklahoma W.C.T.U. (Women's Christian Temperance Union) under the leadership of that courageous woman, Frances Willard, who later united with Susan B. Anthony and the intrepid women fighting for the vote.

With her peculiar single courage after going into Oklahoma at the opening of the territory and filing land, she packed her small bag every week, set out by buck board, into the miserable mining communities where she met in shacks and white steepled church the harried, devout, half-maddened women who saw the miserable pay checks go weekly at the corner saloon, and who attempted to stave off poverty and the disappearance of their husbands by smashing the saloons. They rode on floats in temperance parades with signs reading "Tremble King Alcohol we shall grow up" and "Lips that touch liquor shall never touch mine."

We became a kind of poor landed gentry without connection except with reforms that often met defeat. In my childhood, with the covert fear of the dispossessed, always with women, we set out on dark nights of migration, into the perils and the naked strife and the awful struggle of women, their faces set in rigid discipline so the children could not take terror from them; trekking to another farm, another city in the familiar unmarked trail from Indiana to Illinois into Iowa, into the Dakotas and Minnesota or down into Texas and back again. My grandmother, alone on her last trek, died on a train in the plains.

She always spoke of spunk and grit and barren intestinal courage. I have here a beautiful picture of the New England white house brought to my birthplace, Murray, Iowa. The shadow of a lost day chastely falls from the rigid angles of the straight house, and a tough agile old man stands laughing in the sun while the women rebuke him in their long skirts, which my grandmother wore to her death. The fichu and full bosom, the long sleeves and high at the throat for modesty, were the sign and signal of a last moment of "decency," as she always said. It was the decency of the rural agrarian primitive Christianity, of the flowering of the struggle for democracy.

She never knew that the great fathers Jefferson, Lincoln and Jackson had given way to Carnegie, Morgan and DuPont. She never knew it was so late; too late to turn the fiddle into the lyre, country reel into dancings, the songs of the Cumberland, the Kentucky Campbellites into lyrics and songs of the picket line; too late for the village and prairie dream of an Athens on the Mississippi. New Salem was deserted on the Sangamon (abundant) country; the wooden stool, the axe and the hoe had given way to the giant in the fields. She saw that the village life was gone but she did not see the factory in the field, turning the farmer into the serf of Consolidated peas and corn!

Bitterly she had to oppose her daughters' militant struggle for the vote, or the new industrial developments. But she abandoned the talk of justice and beauty and the rights of all because she could not see how it would come about. She was pragmatic, puritan, realistic in her way. She knew in her bones that steadily, insidiously, and ruthlessly the enemy was winning; the sons of Tubal Cain had outfoxed the angels, and the great tumorous and drunk giants lay across the land. But she held to her passion and moral conviction to the last, and she believed in and held her own human dignity and that of her fellows above reproach.

It was not enough for her first girl child with the tall head and the great asking eyes, born in her lonely room in the New England house in the middle of Iowa.

It is hard to write about Marian Le Sueur, not because she was my mother, but because like myself she was a woman. In many ways her history is suppressed within the history of the man, the history of an oppressed people is hidden in the lies and the agreed-upon myth of its conquerors.

To those who remember her as an independent, aggressive, bold and brilliant woman it is difficult to understand that for each of these distinctions she had to fight most of society, public opinion and the laws of the land. Women especially would like to believe that her talents were God-given. But it was not so. Her anger, her strength, her determination, even her brilliance and her oratory were things she developed, often alone, and struggled and fought for, as much as Frederick Douglass had to struggle to even read. In Texas her husband divorced her on the grounds of dangerous thoughts gleaned from reading books!

You have to think of her in the line of Elizabeth Cady Stanton, Susan B. Anthony, Ameba Bloomer, Carrie Nation, Frances Willard, Lucy Stone, Lucretia Mott, and the later suffragists of whom she was one. These courageous women set a pattern not understood yet, standing in their prim strength, in their sweetness and sobriety against cruel ridicule, moral censure, charges of insanity; for there is no cruelty like that of the oppressor who feels his loss of the bit on those it has been his gain to oppress. "Pine knots as we are," Susan Anthony said. They used the only means open to them—they became orators when it was considered immoral for a woman to speak in public; if she went to meetings she was only to listen and learn. But they could use their constitutional right of petition, and they could tramp up and down, getting signatures for the right to work, to get a divorce, to speak in public, to vote.

If the women in the Christian church did not sit separate from the men it was only an act of courtesy or perhaps a long lost act of rebellion on their part. St. Paul still sat in the front pew saying it is better to marry than to burn, and the heads of the women were covered. She had no legal right to her own property, or to her children; both were the property of the man. A man was responsible legally for the crimes of his wife as he was for his jackass or his cow.

It is touching to think of the young girl, the most brilliant mind in her family, yet a girl. Her father said why weren't you a boy? Her mother said you have too high a forehead for a woman, cover it up—as you covered your legs, your arms, your neck, and all the natural processes of becoming a woman.

The others in the family were jealous because she liked to study. Her brothers said you will never find a husband. The oldest brother, Frank, came back from the race tracks, the darling of his mother, and played practical jokes. At sixteen, after her father's death, she ran away from home to Chicago, bought a red wig and got a job. She did not go to her father's funeral, which my grandmother always said was attended by every "tramp" he had defended.

She went to Drake University, the school of the Christian Church, and was a brilliant mathematician. She went back to Osceola on weekends. The young men who were training to be preachers drove down on Sundays in tandems with spanking horses. A year before her graduation, in her eighteenth year, she married one of them, and they went immediately to his first parish at Boise, Idaho.

The young and frightened wife at a meeting of the Ladies' Aid said that she didn't know if she had been poisoned by something, but she was nauseated. The ladies gave each other significant looks; two were delegated to take the young bride out to tell her privately never to mention again that she was sick because she was going to have a baby. I tell this to show the prudery, the medieval ignorance and darkness.

She came with her husband to the Chicago summer school. She took a course against his wishes on comparative religions, popular and very radical, and to her amazement she found there were other religions, older and as spiritual as the one she knew. She went to school the day before her baby was born.

Her baby died the next summer. I was born the following summer in Murray, Iowa. The rest of these years is the anonymous history of a mother following her husband except that she, with her vigorous and searching mind, studied and read, first William Ellery Channing, the liberals of the church, then Emerson, who remained a great influence, especially the essay on Self-Reliance which is worn out in many collections she still has. She had a son born in Oklahoma at her mother's house, and another son born in San Antonio, Texas.

Then she took one of the leaps of growth for which she was always ready. She welcomed change. She seemed, if she feared it, to always leap that fear and move in new directions. She came to the conclusion entirely outside the experience of her society, that it was a sin to stay with a man you no longer loved. But she had never earned her living. She could not

40

possess any property that did not belong to her husband. She had no vote, no legal status, and divorce in her society was virtually unknown. She faced the poverty of the women she knew who, to raise money even for the church, had to have church suppers, for the only way they could filch money was to put it on the grocery bill, to make cakes and other things and sell them. She and her children were utterly dependent upon the man.

It must be remembered that at this time, outside the professions of nurse and teacher, there were few professions or jobs open to a woman. My mother opened a physical culture studio for women, and here she met Bernarr McFadden who came to lecture to a large audience of women she organized to hear him. She dabbled in real estate and managed a large fig orchard, hiring Mexican workers. She told a liberal lawyer friend that the only way you could make money was to get something where you hire other people and make a profit off their labor. He said all by yourself you've discovered the capitalist system!

She got a bank account and the bank, without asking her, took her money to cover her husband's overdrawn account. She could not get a divorce and was threatened with the loss of her children.

We left everything sitting on the table, our belongings, our books, and left as if we were going on a vacation. But we fled over the "border," to Oklahoma, to my grandmother. Later, Marian's husband got the divorce on the grounds of desertion and her interest in "dangerous literature."

Lecturing by women was considered genteel, even though

41

the platform had become a militant place for the voice of women. Susan Anthony had toured the mining towns and the villages. My mother felt a social responsibility toward women. She had read Ellen Key and found her problem was not her own, but a social problem, and she wanted to speak to women. She had never taken the platform before. She was shy and conventional and intimidated by her long position as a housewife and her isolation from all but church life. Her husband's family said she was insane, that she was a wanton, a "free" woman, a bad woman. My Grandmother gave up her hard-earned position as librarian in the little town of Perry to go back to family raising.

It was a daring and wonderful thing to take the road to talk about the rights of women, in the beginning to stand trembling with nervousness, to be the butt of jokes, to see the frightened, asking eyes of the women who packed the opera houses.

A Missouri paper carried this item in August, 1912:

"The Methodist Church reports a crowded house for Mrs. Wharton's physical culture lecture 'The Glory of Superb Womanhood.' In the evening she occupied the pulpit, speaking of Love and Bread. 'Relating to the sexual science and the science of eugenics, ignorance has been called innocence. Prudery has reigned supreme,' she said. 'Women have been born and reared in ignorance, taught to feel shame toward the most sacred functions of life. Immoralities in and out of wedlock, the terrible white slave traffic, ruined lives, blighted homes, all can be traced to inequality of the sexes, and ignorance'."

Later she barnstormed the little towns, to speak in tents

42

with quartets, horn blowers and juggler acts; but always the farm and village, women waited to speak to her and she saw their eyes, and the children at their skirts, and the weighted and torn bodies.

She became an orator, taking her courage from those eyes. Unequipped and untrained, she studied, made massive notes, overcame her timidity, learned to let her voice go, to compose from the audience which became always the miracle of her speaking. She came to hate exploitation of women by men, at first hating the men, and fiercely struggling to get a place for herself in the world of men.

She started clinics for the miners' children in Oklahoma, but soon found that the wealthy middle-class women who supported them could go only so far, that they were bitted by their husbands and the economic interests of their husbands.

She began to find out that it was not all a matter of love, but of bread also.

She met the editor of the *Kansas City Star,* Billy Williams, who was a friend of Theodore Dreiser. She went down to the hall where the IW.W., the Syndicalists, and the Socialists had school all winter between seasons. Here she went deeper to the roots of women's oppresison and to the oppression of one class by another.

In Chicago she, met Emma Goldman and Eleanor Fitzgerald; she studied anarchism. Later, she met Alexander Berkman who was a great influence on her life and on my own.

But she became a socialist.

IV

The People's College in Fort Scott, where my mother and Arthur Le Sueur went to teach, and where they met, had these aims: to be a college of the working class, to bring education within the reach of every man, woman and child, to teach from the viewpoint of the working class. Not a dollar of profit could ever be made from it by any private individual. There were courses in labor law, labor English, bookkeeping, parliamentary law, and algebra. A magazine, the *Peoples' News,* was edited with the slogan "To remain ignorant is to remain a slave." Eugene V. Debs was the Chancellor and Arthur Le Sueur was the President. The magazine was edited by Arthur Le Sueur and Marian Wharton.

The College was housed in an old mansion in Fort Scott. The town square was once the meeting place of John Brown and his men when they planned forays into Missouri, just over the border. It was located a few miles from Girard, Kansas where the largest farmers' and working class paper was edited.

On the board were Charles Edward Russell, John Work, Charles P. Steinmetz, George Kirkpatrick, Fred Warren, Helen Keller, and many other liberals and Socialists of the period. They envisaged a resident school which would have its own dairies, class rooms, fields, and laboratories. In the meantime, thousands of workers took the correspondence courses. The magazine is full of letters from Missouri sharecroppers, miners in shacks, sailors at sea; from prisons, lonesome cowboys on the range, from foreign born workers struggling with the verb. They received voluminous letters from Comrade Le Sueur and Comrade Wharton urging them to continue, to persevere, to persist, for the working class needed lawyers and speakers and writers.

Marian Wharton wrote a book on workers' English of which Debs said:

"There is no other work on language and its proper use for the benefit of the working class; through its pages also are the apt and illuminating quotations from the speeches and writings of the men and women who have stood in the forefront of the struggle of the ages to destroy tyranny and oppression and emancipate the people. It is a revolutionary textbook, the first issued by the college to constitute the proletarian literature, self-inspired and self-produced, true to truth and free from all ruling-class taint, that is to dispel the darkness and ignorance and superstition among the workers, that will open their eyes and attune their hearts to their common kinship, develop their capacity to think and act for themselves, inspire them with high ideals and resolute purpose and fit them by education and organization for the mental, moral and spiritual mastery of the world."

Out of quotations in this book from revolutionary literature came a demand from the workers for the rest of the quotations, and thus grew the idea for the Little Blue Books, which workers and farmers could carry in their pockets. Letters in the magazine came from the moonlight Kentucky schools, from the weekend schools in Oklahoma where people came and tented out and studied in the open.

It was a few years of wonderful activity. The College grew, they planned travelling libraries, and plans for village forums appeared in the magazine.

Comrade Le Sueur and Comrade Wharton, come such divers paths and yet similar paths of the mind and the idea, were married.

The first world war "broke out."

The Socialist convention of 1914 was against the war. The St. Louis convention, faced with American entry into world war, split on the question. John Spargo introduced a pro-war resolution. The opposing left resolution introduced by Hillquit and supported by C. E. Ruthenberg and Alfred Wagenknecht was passed. The Socialist Party split. The rank and file led strikes, the membership increased. There were trials of those opposed to the draft, the *Masses* trial, the trial of the anarchists. The I.W.W. in June 1916, opened a strike in Minnesota where sixteen thousand miners walked out. They organized timber workers in Everett, Washington. Five members were killed. They had a strike in the copper country, the year we declared war, involving twenty-four thousand miners; in Bisbee, Arizona two thousand miners were seized and taken out to the desert. Frank Little was kidnapped and hanged in Butte.

The "liberal" Wilson, elected on a plank to keep America out of the war, got us into war five months later, and Congress adopted a body of reactionary legislation: the Espionage Act, Trading with the Enemy Act, Conscription Act, and anti-sedition and anti-syndicalism laws. Raids were made on the I.W.W., private homes broken into, two thousand I.W.W. members arrested. Non-Partisan League organizers were tarred and feathered.

Arthur and Marian Le Sueur now came to St. Paul, Minnesota to work in the Non-Partisan League and to defend the many civil rights cases.

They had nothing, and they started over, Arthur at the age of fifty, and Marian ten years younger. With Marian's three children and her mother they lived on Dayton Avenue in St. Paul. With their capacity for beginning life over completely, Marian studied law and stenography and became his secretary. They were also educational directors for the Non-Partisan League and Arthur served as legal consultant and aided in writing many of the laws of North Dakota. The League had come to power in 1915, was growing in Minnesota and Montana and the bordering states. Like the I.W.W. it grew during the war years.

Arthur defended the victims of the free speech fights, the foreign born, the farmers whose houses were painted yellow, the co-op leaders who were indicted, the I.W.W.'s. He himself was threatened, and like Charles Lindbergh Sr., barely escaped many acts of violence.

They seemed at this time to precariously walk the tightrope of a balance of the left forces within the cage of capitalist relationships. Possibly underestimating the forces of imperialism, they held as well as they could to the old forms of democracy, within the body of the people's unflagging struggle. They had a canny and precise patience and estimate of not going too far ahead of these struggles.

They moved out fearlessly and any moderation was due to their theoretical limitations, to the feeling of collective skill and survival; they moved the way they felt the national emergency and need. They were athletic and bold, but like many others on the left, they underestimated the power and intention of the American workers.

Arthur urged the I.W.W. not to oppose the war outright, fearing bloody reprisals. He felt the League under Townley was endangered by bossism and the reckless use of their economic power, and the egomania of its political leaders. He incurred the wrath of Haywood by his belief that it was not the time on the range to come head on with the legal powers in defense of the miners accused of murder in the range strike, that a deal should be made to give them life terms, and after the hysteria had subsided, to get a commutation of the sentence. He did not believe in "mass trials." Still a captive of his faith in Blackstone legalism, he believed the law could win. He boasted that none of his cases went to jail during this period. He relied on his own brilliance and court skill.

Marian found herself back in the cage of marriage she had tried to escape. She was no longer Comrade Wharton, head of the English Department, with her own house and life. She was now doubly servant; she went to the office at nine after getting her children off, she came back at four, cleaned house, and got supper; in the evening she ran up and down between the apartment they occupied upstairs and the children's lessons in the front room.

She helped organize with another feminist a nursing service for mothers; she worked in the defense of Tom Mooney, and for suffrage for women.

In this period Victor Berger was excluded from his seat in Congress. Robert M. La Follette cast his one vote against the war. Debs went to jail. Eight hundred were convicted under the Espionage and Sedition law without one iota of proof of any injury to the miltary services.

Despite the suppression, there were more strikes from the beginning of the war to the time of the Palmer Raids than in any period in the history of America. On Lincoln's birthday in 1919, fifty-four I.W.W.s were ordered deported. On January 2, 1920, ten thousand people were arrested. Men and women were dragged from their beds; strike-breaking recruits cavorted in masks of Marx and Debs which they had torn from workers' halls. One Judge described them as "a mob made up of government officials acting under instructions from the Department of Justice." The arrested passed through the streets in handcuffs; musicians and dancers were seized, students of a geography class. Transports stood at the ports ready for them.

In their defense Arthur went to Washington and asked Louis Post, Assistant Secretary of Labor, to stand up and smash these illegal cases of J. Edgar Hoover. "I'll be impeached," he said. "Stand up and you'll be a hero," Arthur told him. He did get the courage to dismiss the cases and the Secretary of Labor ruled that a membership card was insufficient evidence and that Communist Labor Party members were exempt from the deportation statute. Impeachment charges were made against Post but he stood his ground, and the illegality of the raids was exposed to the public.

Arthur printed a brochure exposing the illegal practices of the U.S. Department of Justice, the illegality of their arrest of aliens, and the violation of the Fourth and Fifth, as well as the First and Eighth amendments to the Constitution.

This was a great influence that changed our lives:

One day a short, elegant little man with blue eyes and a goatee sat in our front room, where people crowded in, around the walls, on the floor and up the stairway. He was Lincoln Steffens returned from a new world experiment. He had come back to speak secretly and tell about the new Russian revolution. He had gone there as Mr. Wilson's ambassador, and when he returned all his papers were seized and he was ordered not to speak publicly of the new Soviet Union. Wilson was ready to betray the thousands of workers who had laid down their guns on the German front to show him that they meant peace. He was following the dastardly plan of Wall Street for intervention.

We listened for hours as he told of this and answered questions, and a new world opened before us in that little wooden house on Dayton Avenue. Not a listener ever forgot the picture he gave of a man named Lenin, of the workers with guns in their hands, of the setting up of a new government.

A new era had begun.

V

In October, 1919 the Non-Partisan League had two hundred and forty thousand members, three representatives in Congress, and was organized in thirteen states. The forces marshalled against the League were the new imperialist forces consolidated by the end of the war. The whales of Britain, France and America had swallowed the smaller whales. They employed every measure to destroy the political power that had successfully threatened the huge profits of the money lenders with their roots in Wall Street, menaced the great railroad companies linked with the packing house combinations. With co-op and state owned elevators, they had struck at the great grain combines and the flour milling interests. The Hail Insurance Act menaced the profits and grip of the Insurance companies. Other bills, Workmens' Compensation Laws, strict inspection of mines, referendum and recall laws, and the publishing of their own textbooks, made a direct attack upon the great banks and controlling interests in America.

In terror, reaction sought to crack down on the left. All the forces of press and pulpit, of injunction and chicanery, were put to work. They tried to reorganize the primaries, to impugn the state-owned bank; the crack-down of the Palmer raids aimed at the destruction of the steel strike of 1919. They wanted to

51

smash the newly formed Communist Party, the trade unions, the third party organizations.

Arthur Le Sueur sat in St. Paul and chewed cigars and paced the streets and tried to get a voice in North Dakota. The liberals who thought the Non-Partisan League was utopia trekked back through St. Paul. Many of them literally died. Bitterness gathered. Impoverished and disillusioned, they came back with their children, and many stayed at our house. The men wilted away as if the end of the world had come. Some went into business, became rich; some became stool pigeons. A well-known writer who stayed at our house turned informer. When Arthur tried to get a visa to go as a farmers' delegate to the meeting at Versailles where he wanted to present the plan he and Marian had written for a United Nations, Mr. Wilson refused him and told him to go back to the farmers. "Pshaw, pshaw," Wilson said. "Do not speak of that of which you know nothing."

Anger gathered in his fist.

He was attacked, red baited. On my table is a pamphlet issued in Minneapolis in 1920 "exposing" the leaders of the Non-Partisan League, a scurrilous document, forerunner of Stassen's "Communists or Catspaws?" in the 1938 campaign.

A mass campaign for amnesty released Debs in 1921. The other I.W.W.s were released in 1922. The 'twenties began. It was hard to make a living. The Socialist Party had split. The Communist Party was born. Arthur and Marian did not go in that direction. They continued in the growing farmer-labor movement, culminating in the independent candidacy in 1924 of Bob LaFollette for the presidency. This was the greatest effort of the rank and file towards an independent party. Into it came the Non-Partisan League, the Committee of Forty-eight, the Plumb Plan movement, an organization of the railroads, and the Farmer-Labor Party. The N.A.A.C.P. endorsed LaFollette.

So they entered a new life, a new struggle.

Like everyone in the period between the 'twenties and the crash they tried to make a "nest egg" by starting a chicken ranch in California which, like most, was lost to the mortgage. They had no stomach for the "private umbrella."

The crash came.

We all came to live together and pool our resources in a house on Harriet Avenue in Minneapolis. There was no more private living. We had no key to our door or latch to the ice box. My mother and I came down in the morning and looked on the couch to see what fresh emissary from the east or west would be asleep in the living room. Sometimes we didn't know them. Word had gone out to some Oklahoma ballad singer, some marine organizer, W.P.A. worker, or striker without a bed.

Marian had become a grandmother with as fierce a stroke as she became everything. My children lived there.

We argued. There was talk from the time anyone's feet hit the floor in early morning. All did not agree. No one had to agree. Children spoke at the table also. Marian was writing a book on all the derivations of words from the Latin, Greek and Anglo-Saxon. Arthur was elected to the school board. He was also fighting the wartime back pay cases of the steel workers, cases which he fought the rest of his life.

I was writing. My brother was beginning to be a painter, and had a wife and later a child. My other brother and his wife were working. There was fiddle-playing and singing around the upright piano in the hall. Marian was cooking and figuring to feed everyone on forty-one cents a day.

My daughter said that the wonder of the household was that nobody seemed to feel they were in a depression. We had the happy security of birds. We never worried. It seems we had about the same struggle, come depression or boom. We had the same amount of nothing, of struggle, richness and growth. Arthur was writing an essay on banking. Marian studied Hindu philosophy. This search went on, always passionate, indefatigable, tempestuous.

My daughter said it never occurred to her that you must ever give up your ideas for economic security. There seemed never to be that choice. Security seemed to be something you had more of by being true to your beliefs. A house was only a house—it was nothing you gave your life to have, or sacrificed an idea to protect; the same with a job.

When Arthur was up for re-election as Judge, the Minneapolis syndicate stopped him on the court-house steps and told him that if he wanted to be elected he would have to play with them. He never stopped walking. He did not have to make a decision. When he told it at home we only laughed that *anybody* should think they could proposition Arthur who, as Marian always said, "leaned over backwards."

The Farmer-Labor Party came into power with Floyd Olson as governor, and Marian was appointed to the Planning Board and the Board of Education. Her organizational and educational talents came the nearest to being used to their capacity in this period. Her contribution to the planning board was the pioneer work on public power which led to the Missouri Valley Authority and rural electrification program.

Arthur had just won the case against the Telephone Company.

The big strike of '34 broke the Citizens' Alliance grip on Minneapolis labor.

They worked in the Farmer-Labor Association, the educational base of the Farmer-Labor Party, and they helped to edit the party's newspaper, the *Leader*.

The Spanish war moved them deeply; delegates from the Spanish republic stayed at our house. There was the question of state power which Arthur had known in the Dakotas, in the strike in Minneapolis when Olson raided the headquarters of the right, left and middle!

The Spanish war was lost. Olson died, Benson was governor. Arthur Le Sueur was his appointee as Municipal Judge. It is remembered by the workers of Minneapolis that for a short time a judge sat on the bench who valued human life above property. When the election came up, his picture was in the windows of the working class districts. He was defeated by the opposition of the Bar Association and the Syndicate and a lot of money.

To live they had to go to a rooming house. Arthur aged. Half blind and sick, he practiced law to the end. He was in court in December, 1949 at the age of eighty-three. He took sick. He had cancer. Marian fought for him against the powers of darkness.

In his death-hours the Rabelaisian humor, the whimsy of his stories of Johnny Hoppergrass made his room a place of warmth and strength. The deep demos in him, the humor, the generosity were there—"Death can't scare me or buy me either. . . . It doesn't look like we can get a change of venue from this court. . . . There will be blood on the snow if fascism wins now." The deep reflective pools hidden in him now were expressed, horizon strengths and the full, rich nature in the service of others, eruptions, Rabelaisian jokes woven into his will to fight, often individualistic, a bull in the china shop. Often he fought too much alone, but an enemy of the worker and the farm women he remembered, and the cold gyppo camps, with the trees popping and injustice poured like a torrent bursting a man's heart, worse than a log jam, when docility turned to danger and the lamb roared—these things were never forgotten or lost in him. "Plot with all your wits, outwit the assassins, take it to the higher court"—and death skulked off like a corporation lawyer.

Such men with colossal egos and lonely fighting strength will not be again. He would hope that there would be less mutilated men and better men, and that when there are, they would stand on his shoulders. In his files are ponderous and careful letters written to the President of Mexico, to Spanish refugees, an answer to any cry.

When he was ruled out in the court of death, with no appeal and no higher court, he said, "Do not think the fight has diminished or that there are not the sinewed and stronger fighters coming on."

Alone, he pulled out the thread of his last breath, handed us the courage, and died March 19, 1950.

"People like the Le Sueurs who serve the public with such loyalty and fidelity are never praised or commended by the reptile press, but instead they are held up to ridicule and derided. So the common people find their way to honor them. Honored guests at a public reception which packed a large hall, they, who have taken so much abuse and condemnation from sources that live on the backs of the people, sat in the places of honor and heard the people speak out to laud and praise them, straight from the heart."

> From the *Labor Review* on the occasion of the reception for the Le Sueurs November 11, 1943.

"O hope and faith!
O aching close of exiled patriots' lives!
O many a sicken'd heart!
Turn back unto this day, and make yourselves afresh."
                                    Whitman

VI

There's many a man buried in the Middle West with the picture of Ingersoll on his coffin and the words said over him: "Say not they die whose heart beats with the world's great heart." Much was said at the funeral of Joe Hill in Chicago, when the choruses stood on the hills singing all the afternoon, and his comrades spoke in every tongue, and his ashes were divided and sent to every nation of the world (except the State of Utah that killed him) and on the following May Day all over the earth they were scattered in the wind.

Arthur Le Sueur himself told many a story of his own

officiations at funerals, of driving out, himself and the preacher called by the wife—who most often was left behind in her husband's ideological struggle. The preacher was often as afraid of him as he would have been of the devil, for much superstition was thrown with the tar about the awful "atheists" and the midnight rites and terrors of their beliefs. Arthur said that once the preacher was shivering and rolling his eyes, and sitting as far over as he could, and at last he asked what the atheists did at funerals. Arthur said: "You better see that the coffin's closed before you speak because we bury them face down so they can give a last salute to the preachers!"

These memorials to Marian and Arthur Le Sueur are given here both as a history and a pattern for memorials of those who have been, not only individuals, but collective forces in the city and the country.

The funeral has long been an instrument also of conveying history that has become hidden, of subtly informing the young, and of mining and blowing the mineral of collective poetry and courage. In Ireland during the uprising of 1798 funerals were political meetings and often as not the coffin contained pamphlets of the Rights of Man instead of a corpse. Funerals were the gathering of the bards, the poets, the historians; and the Irish wakes really originated as fires of collective history and language and information of the struggle. There were poets who carried this history walking on their two legs, and handed it down in the native, forbidden tongue.

In these memorials a pattern is made which can be followed by others. This is collective history told by the people who lived it. Memory in America suffers amnesia. Here the memory is blown from the ashes and glows in the city. Here not only the leaders of movements, but all speak. It would be good if they could continue all day and all night for the tongue is loosened not by the grapes' ferment in time, but by the ferment of memory in the mind and heart of men and women who have struggled in danger together, who have stood against the lions of power even for a moment. It is not the dead alone who are honored, but the living. Particularly the youth take the strength of the fallen tree.

These memorials are arranged chronologically and give a sense of continuity of history, and of inheritance. Let others rise from the audience to speak also. Let poetry be written and spoken. Let the singers come and the children. Let there be strength and joy and a firm grasp of the future; not the threat of death for all, but only the threat of having lived meekly, in private despair, voiceless and mute.

Arthur Le Sueur's memorial was held in the Unitarian Church on a cold day. But the hall was packed and the faces were those familiar in many years of the life of the city; engineers, teachers, labor leaders, lawyers, students, old workers from old struggles. A young man played a medley of songs, author's favorites—*Lindy Lou, The Miner's Daughter, The People's Flag Is Deepest Red, The International, Pie in the Sky, Sweet Betsy from Pike, Solidarity*. Meridel Le Sueur was chairman and opened the Memorial.

"We are gathered here in a living group, known and loved by our father, husband, friend, comrade, grandfather and great-

60

grandfather, his wife, his children, grand-children, his comrade in arms.

"He is a stranger to any solemnity on this day. He left us a great heritage, an inheritance, a will we will read this day. He bequeathed to us the belief in the vast human possibilities of man, the love of our land, and the courage to claim both; the only instrument against the atom bomb, the potentials and strength of believing man and women."

Joseph Gilbert, eighty-six years old, still writing a column for the Co-op magazine, was the first speaker. He said Arthur Le Sueur could have been of the worldly great but that he said, with Whitman, "I'll accept nothing that all cannot have upon the same terms," that his love of humanity was greater than personal gain.

"We hear a good deal about democracy today but we give only lip service.

"The real democrat is the one who is willing to think not of himself, not to care about the plaudits of the crowd, but to serve humanity as a whole, that's the thing.

"He championed the cause of the people.

"He didn't hesitate in those days when the word Socialist was like the word Communist today.

"He was great in the real sense of the term great. He lost sight of the word *self* entirely and when we honor him today we honor ourselves for having recognized in him those qualities which the world so badly needs.

"A man like this is willing to cast career aside and cares nothing except to serve his fellow men.

"I am an old man and I see the great value of a social life is that you do not die, the spirit lives on and inspires the rising generations to carry on the work which they have done.

61

The world's a stage but how shall we act? Shall we be little people who think of themselves or shall we be that type who uses his ability, his energy, his talent to make the world a better place in which to live?

"That is the measure of a great man and that is the kind of man Arthur Le Sueur was."

Another middle western teacher, with the snows of years, E. Dudley Parsons, whose father came from England to preach equality in the south before the Civil War, an historian of the city, a man who fearlessly lived his beliefs, said:

"He is not lost to us, since his energy and vital thinking has become part of us and we shall not fail to transmit his values to those whom we in turn touch. This is the splendor of eternal and universal life.

"It was meet that the judge lived to see a marvelous life emerging in new and constructive forms in all parts of the world and to know his contribution to this universal expression. He is honored in the victory of great masses of mankind over the forces that have heretofore exploited them.

"He had the training and ability that the great financial powers like to employ to exploit the workers and farmers, but he chose to serve the universal life and placed his powers at the disposal of the workers and farmers who are the majority and not in the service of the sixty families. As a Socialist when it was a horrendous word he helped to make the grand history of the North Dakota reform movement. A mayor of Minot, he fought for civil rights for all. He entered into the life of our city, as school board member where he fought across the table with the racketeers, the enemies of education.

"As municipal judge he brought to the bench the sympathy for the men and women appearing before him that gave them a new sense of justice.

"When he should have rested he was forced to enter private practice, he became a center for the discouraged, the confused contenders. How often I have been sent from his office uplifted, re-dedicated.

"He was part of a great structure that will go on building.

"We feel his vital pulse.

"We have become his heirs to a rich legacy."

There followed tributes from the C.I.O., the A.F. of L., the Teachers and Janitors Unions, telegrams from all over the United States. Bob Kramer, editor of the A.F. of L. paper, the *Labor Review,* brought expression of sorrow from the central body of the Minneapolis Central Labor Union:

"Arthur Le Sueur always appeared to me as a people's lawyer. He went to the defense of any sincere citizen regardless of whether he agreed with him or not. We don't realize how these men like Art affected and moved not only this part of the country but the whole nation and the whole world. The British Premier at a luncheon here said that they watched this part of the country because here originated more political ideas and more militancy than in any other part of the world.

"Art Le Sueur was one of the great contributors to that progress. He knew from the standpoint of a worker how it felt to be earning your living from a wage.

"He knew from the standpoint of a farmer how the palaces on the hill grew out of hardship and suffering of the farmers who lived in the shacks.

"I think the greatest thing he did was to bring the farmers and workers closer together.

"For the sacrifices he made and the life he lived for the progress and defense and the welfare of the common man, the

Central Labor Union and its sixty thousand affiliates express their everlasting gratitude."

Teachers remembered how he fought corruption in the schools, helped expose the Silver Shirts, raised the pay of the teachers. Mercedes Nelson of the Women's Teachers Federation paid homage to his persistence; his stubbornness and daring in a fight, his support of education for the common people; how he fought, almost alone, the racketeering, the irregularities of orders, pay for teachers, security of tenure.

"I can think of nothing," she said, "that would please Mr. Le Sueur more than to pledge all union teachers to carry on, united for the schools, for the best education for all children of the world, to make our education a force for democracy that he envisioned."

Ralph Ahlstrom, another teacher, said Arthur was like the ancient Athenian who went about the streets puncturing sophistry.

"A great man has gone from our midst," he said. "His was the kind of greatness which stemmed from a dedication of life. From the day he turned his back on the defense of corporate wealth and resigned as counsel for a great railroad he never veered from his course. He had complete faith in the idea that a scientifically socialized world would free mankind from most of its bigotry, intolerance, superstition and cruelty."

Others spoke: Jack Lieberman, who knew him in Minot during the I.W.W. struggles; Vienna Johnson who had been raised on the range during the early strikes, and was later editor of the *Farmer Labor Leader,* spoke of the early strikes in her girlhood and his defense of the miners and the I.W.W. She said:

"When Arthur Le Sueur believed in the righteousness of a cause he was absolutely fearless.

"But I will always think of them as members of a splendid team, a partnership, the team of Marian and Arthur.

"While they traveled this rough, rugged road that must be trod by the men and women who labor for mankind, there must have been times that they found solace in the fact that they were travelling the same road together. It must be a very heart-warming experience to find a mate who understands your beliefs, who has the same principles, two people who have dedicated themselves to the same great goals.

"The relationship of Marian and Arthur Le Sueur was a rich, rare relationship from which they gained as individuals and from which society as a whole benefited."

So the afternoon waned, was no longer cold, the room was touched with no winter sun. Reverend Hester, a preacher from an Abolitionist family, read a poem he had written.

"When the goin's tough, just look up
and see us grinning with Gene Debs
as with spur and saddle and bit in his mouth we ride the Wall Street donkey in Canaan,
Then having tied our jackass outside the gates, where such animals dare not enter, we go in and join the happy workers."

He refers here to a favorite story of Arthur's about Gene Debs. On his way to heaven he met a sad creature who couldn't get in. It was Mr. Rockefeller being sent down to hell. He begged Debs to help him get into heaven, saying he was always a kindly man. Debs said he didn't have any influence with the Union of Angels but Rockefeller said, "I'll get on my hands and knees and you pretend you are riding into heaven." So Debs got on Rockefeller's back and they got to the gates of heaven and St. Peter roared out a welcome to Debs, "We've been waiting for you, Eugene. The Pullman Porters Union of Angels have arranged a big banquet. Get down off that jackass you're riding and come in!"

The last speaker was a man who had come as a youth into Arthur's office, and had been secretary to both Governor Olson and Governor Benson. Roger Rutchick said:

"He was a true product of the American frontier, born long before its disappearance, and grew under its potent spell. He was no mere good-doer. When he was the fighting mayor of Minot life was rugged. He represented all that was good in the frontier, and he resented the forces which arose in American life as the frontier disappeared forever.

"He hated the growth of monopoly.

"He was like Governor Altgeld and others of those days.

"He resented the impoverishment of the farmer and the injustices.

"He was outraged by the cruel exploitation of the workers of our land.

"Fortunate for us he lived in the time, and at the place, where his particular talents could be turned to Humanity's advantage."

Sitting in the front row were Arthur's son, his son's son, his grand-daughter and her husband, a young attorney just passed the bar, Kenneth Tilsen, who spoke extemporaneously:

66

"There is little I can add to what has been said for I knew him but a short time. But he hammered into my mind the idea that the law is a double-edged sword, one edge the instrument of property, the other to be used in defense of the people. He pointed out that the law was what we made it. . . .

"I can say that Arthur Le Sueur has left a path that I am going to attempt to follow and I hope that I will never turn my back on the people in the way that he never turned his back on them."

Meridel Le Sueur spoke the requiem:
"Whom shall we address in saying now farewell?
He is a stranger to any solemn day,
He who travelled a short while towards the sun
And left the air signed with his struggle.

He knew how greed and power can
Annul the dignity of man.
He was one of us who said
Our children have what we missed
We gather lightning in our fist.

Whom shall we address then in saying now farewell?
To whom do we bring flowers to place around him now?
For wherever there is struggle he will be!
He was our hunger and our need
He will be in our strong step marching against all locks.

What is your terror if he is not fighting it?
All those who fall now shall be spoken of among
    the people,
They shall live again in deeds,

For none shall die who have the future in them.
For over him there stands the deathless purpose.

Our memory will not pass with this day's singing,
For we raise monument with fists harder with the
    weapons
He helped forge.
He was of the men
Between the thunder and the lightning crash
Who dreamed.
One of the bright warriors who believed that an
    army came after him
And that we built firm upon the light of time.
He was a runner as we are
And we pick up the torch.

He was of the uncompleted lovers of the future
    and of freedom.

And wherever and whenever today they fall
Over the vast and turbulent earth
We lock arms closer over their going.
And when that great new family of freedom's born,
The family of the free
There will be a peaceful word
With which to remember thee."

"In a government which imprisons any unjustly, the true place of a just man is also in prison.

"Loyalty is a word which has worked vast hard, for it has been made to trick men into being loyal to a thousand inequities. The first thing I want to teach is disloyalty. This will beget independence—which is loyalty to one's best self and principles and this is often disloyalty to the general idols and fetishes.

"Treason! Where does such treason take its rise? I cannot help thinking of you as you deserve, ye governments. Can you dry up the fountains of thought? High treason, when it is resistance to tyranny below has its origin in, and is first committed by the power that makes and forever re-creates man. When you have caught and hung all these human rebels, you have accomplished nothing but your own guilt."

Henry Thoreau

VII

Marian Le Sueur was part of a broken team now. Death is a change into a new life, and adjustment to a new idea. She and Arthur had scarcely had a meal apart or spent a day without his return at four on the bus, and the evenings together, and since his blindness the reading together. The amazing things about her were the rebirths, the transformations, the courage to leap into new forms. Now she had to live in single harness, reorganize her life and the idea, walk out now blindfolded into the final change.

It was not easy, as Irene Paull says in her poem to my

mother, she was not a stereotype of a nice woman; her mother-hood, her love, her wifehood was fierce, possessive, often devouring but also strong, ejective, and the struggle for her was always full of the risk and passion of the vitality of change.

When she couldn't sleep the doctors said, take a barbital —what can you do after seventy, ride out the decay in a half-sleep. But not for her who would scarcely take a drink of wine, wanting to always know what she was doing, to jump the ball when possible. So she didn't take it but rode out the grief. The four years now were in some ways the years of her most tremendous growth. Tempestuous and doggedly honest, she faced many of the things in her personal life without ego, with the scalpel of her piercing mind. It was a great thing to see and expose the hideous cultural idea of the end of growth, and its limitations.

In 1952, in the midst of the repression and terror, she ran for Senator on the Progressive Party ticket to protest the Korean war and give voice to the almost silent northwest.

She was seventy-five years old, had still to make her living; she went to the Progressive Party office every morning, wrote speeches, toured the countryside, spoke in the houses and the little halls again, recorded radio programs, mimeographed leaflets for the fair. She said it might shorten her life, but it was worth it.

She saw in China the subduing of capitalism, the use of power for the worker and farmer, the emancipation of women. She wanted to go to the Peace Conference in Poland. She wanted above everything to see the New Democracies. This was one thing she did not do. She could not afford it.

She enjoyed her grandchildren, her great-grandchildren. She saw her granddaughter working in a factory and she thought she should have done that, gotten close to the working woman. The woman at the machine knew what industrialism was. My mother did not always understand other women, their timidity and fright, but she came to love the women in the Farmer-Labor movement. She broke the molds, the stereotypes of a woman. Being beautiful physically she struggled to overcome the power and prestige our society gives that beauty, and develop the mind. With no skill and no training she had to batter everything out of the wilderness of oppression, of being a woman, and was often angered by her unjust helplessness. In all her political struggles she was never given a political office; like most women she was relegated to the hot dish, the dishwashing, at most the column in the paper and her magnificent oratory.

But as my daughters said, we never had a nervous breakdown. It was very un-neurotic because there were no choices. It was very simple, they say. You did what was right. You never were tempted by the easy road, in fact, it was suspect. You never got bogged down. The expedient was out before you began. A house was just a house. Measured against your own integrity it was nothing; the same with dollars. Money is only money, beans tonight and steak tomorrow. So long as you can look yourself in the eye.

Arthur was the same, they say. You didn't have to worry if he would buckle under to the school board, "go along," as the saying is. He fought them all, told them where they could go, came home, ate a big supper, told a Johnny Hoppergrass story, played Go-to-the-bank with the kids. The world was just a world, you didn't sell your soul for it. It was just an old courthouse, an old judgeship. It was your courthouse and your city and your nation, too. You had some responsibility to it. Just a government, your government, and you could change it. A great democratic thing, they say.

We'll never fear loss of a job, or a depression; we never feared losing anything, did we? We lost everything time and again for our beliefs. It's a hard time now for jobs. A little expediency, a little silence, a little "cooperation" could get you a job, publish your books, make you rich.

The only practical life is the one where you live simply, stick to your guns, as Arthur said. A certain Calvinist diablerie came into it. The easy-roaders sold out, sickened, died, were lost, did not grow, participate, see the changing world.

The day before her operation, when she was seventy-six, my mother wrote to her children:

"Death can be only change. Death is a friend opening a door. Don't grieve for me. I've had a wonderful life of struggle and growing. When I look back upon our history I see the struggle of the people for the American dream against the kings of power. These forebears of ours who never lowered their flag, pass it on to us. This is our heritage. This is our day to fight.

"The American destiny is what our fathers dreamed, a land of the free, and the home of the brave; but only the brave can be free. Science has made the dream of today's reality for all the earth if we have the courage and vision to build it. American Democracy must furnish the engineers of world plenty—the builders of world peace and freedom.

72

"I do believe in the oneness and eternalness of life. Arthur and I like Moses, looked across time to the future of the full life in freedom and brotherhood for all. Our children, grandchildren and great-grandchildren will see that future.

"My life has been a rich life, lived in struggle to grow and understand and help build a world where every man and woman could have equal opportunity to be his rich full self."

She had a vision in her death. She was fearless for us all. And she had a vision. She was at a great conclave held in the prairies, and the plains, rising to the Rockies, were covered with singers of every nationality. As the Indians used to always dream, from the roads leading from north, east, south and west came the red, white, black and yellow peoples, all meeting under the great sky tree of the plains. At this meeting, under the canopy of the sky, the leaders stood. The speaker was Mao Tse-tung. And he was calling out the names of the people's leaders and they rose and came forward in a great light from every country of the world. As they came forward great singing was heard. Then he called out "America," and the very hills sang and resounded, and among those called, of a great number, Mao called the names of "Marian and Arthur Le Sueur, buried in the cornerstone of the future, the seed of our mighty land!"

VIII

"Dark Mother, gliding near, I chant thee a chant of
    fullest welcome.
From me glad serenades, adornments and feasting,
And the sights of the open landscape and the high
    spread sky are fitting,
And life and the fields and the huge and thoughtful
    spring.
Over the fields and the prairies wide,
Over the dense packed cities I float this carol of joy,
    with joy to thee."

Rachel, the granddaughter of Marian Le Sueur, on a clear day, February 14, 1954, with these words of Whitman opened the Memorial. The sky passed over the great windows of the new Unitarian Church, filled with the faces of those known for many a year to her; farmers from the north, the strong face of the mother, the wife, garment workers, labor leaders, all gathering in the Sunday afternoon in the great city.

And Rachel's voice ringing out in the full rich air of friends:

"The great city in this day is not the costliest building,
    nor the place where money is plentiest,
Where the city stands with the brawniest breed of
    patriots, and fighters and orators.

The city is beloved by those who fight the kings of
    power and comrades love and understand them.
Where the slave ceases and the master of the slave ceases.
There the populace rise at once against the audacity of
    elected persons.
Where fierce men and women pour forth.
Where the citizen is the head and ideal.
Where the city of the faithfullest friends stands.
Where the city of the healthiest father stands.
Where the city of the best bodied mothers stands.
There the great city stands and endures."

Fred Ptashne, of the Progressive Party, was chairman, and
after the song *If I Had a Hammer* was sung, he said:
"This is the kind of Memorial Marian Le Sueur herself
would have wanted us to have, a gathering of friends, associates
in the Co-op movement, Farmer-Labor Party, the Democratic
Farmer-Labor Party — farmers, miners, old co-workers, her
children, great-grandchildren."

He gave a short history of her life, ending with her
magnificent campaign against the war in Korea.
Rachel continued:

"What do you think endures?
 Do you think the great city endures?
 Or a teeming manufacturing state, or a prepared
    constitution, or hotels of granite or iron?
 Away . . . these are not to be cherished for themselves,
 The show passes, all does well enough,
 All goes very well till one flash of defiance.
 The great city is that which has the greatest man
    or woman.

If it be a few ragged huts, it is still the greatest city
    in the whole world.

How beggarly appear arguments before a defiant deed.
How the floridness of the materials of cities shrivels
    before a man's or a woman's look.
All waits or goes by default till a strong being appears.
A strong being is the proof of the race, of the ability of
    the universe;
When he or she appears, materials are overawed.
The disputes of the soul stop.
The old customs and phrases are confronted, turned
    back, or laid away.
What is your money making now? What can it do now?
What is your respectability now?
What are your theology, tuition, society, traditions,
    statute books now?

There is the man or woman who stands against the slavers.
I see a woman who stood in the fruitage of her nation.
Partook of the destiny and fulfillment.
Of the great prairies rising, hooded, hidden often but
    rising.
I see those who live in the corner stone of the future.
I see those in any land who have died for a good cause.
The seed is spare, nevertheless the crop shall never run
    out."

Fred Ptashne stood in the high pulpit and looked at the
circle of friends who sat on the platform, the sun striking on
them through the great windows. The old faces were there
with the deep lines, but the young, strong faces too. He intro-

duced Dan Collins, a small Irishman with a fine, colored face and white hair, who had been four decades in the Co-op movement, had in the old Model Ts driven into the villages to organize a Co-op, sometimes with two men coming to the first meeting.

Dan Collins said:

"There are those who place life itself as the earth's most choice possession. These are they who challenged every evil which would curb life or spoil its fullest expression. She was of those who give loyal support to every good effort to make life and living noble and full of meaning.

"As our world becomes smaller and smaller; as the fear and destruction become more desperate, as the tides of world war and peace sharpen and the destiny of mankind hangs in the balance we could all well bow our heads in humble gratitude that the past has had enough souls to hold the line for human emancipation and equality. To this task, to this faith, to this idealism our friend, Marian Le Sueur, gave her full measure of devotion."

The chairman introduced another oldtimer who went to jail in the first World War, had given his life to Socialism and the co-operative movement and was now edging toward ninety years, an Englishman come as a young man to this country:

"We are gathered today to honor a woman who might be classed as a pioneer in bringing in a new world. Women are playing a greater part in the world of today. Today we honor ourselves proving that we are united in a common purpose.

"She was one of the great women in her time, always in the forefront of the struggle. We need more women like her.

I have lived a long time and have done many of the same kinds of things Marian Le Sueur did, but I realize that it is even harder for a woman to be a radical than it is for a man. She had more to contend against but she never flinched in the great struggle to raise the position of women to an equal plane."

Mr. Ptashne said there were those who remembered her as a youthful leader in the time of Debs, others with the I.W.W. and the struggle for civil liberties; still others remembered the women who picketed the White House and were jailed in the suffrage fight. The next speaker was a woman who had been half a century in our community, the wife of one of the first liberal legislators, Mrs. Stockwell. Being herself near ninety she sat to speak, without notes.

"Marian Le Sueur was active in civil affairs long before the passage of the nineteenth amendment which gave the vote to women. She had discovered laws were unjust and became an active suffragette and worked to correct these laws. She was of the inspiration of Lucretia Mott, Susan Anthony, and later Anna Howard Shaw. All of these women not only abhorred injustice but had the determination to do something about it. I think that I might say that the key to her activities was education of the people. She was impatient of the slow marching of time. I might call her the impatient crusader. Her fine mind, her courage, her gift of expression made her a power. Her intense feeling on every question made her a power with the workers. We will miss her mind, her courage, her remarkable gift of expression. Her passing is a loss to this community and this state."

Vienna Johnson was a long time friend, herself an editor of the *Leader*. She dedicated this poem to Marian Le Sueur.

"We, the men and women of the North Star State, who
      knew you, loved you,
Pause today, to reflect,
To recall your achievements,
Your dynamic contributions to all causes dedicated to
      the welfare of mankind.

O, beloved friend, you were as versatile as the seasons
      of our great State.
Within you stirred the promise of spring
Within you surged the fulfillment of summer
Within you throbbed the compassion of autumn
And the great vigor of our winter flowed through your
      veins.

So . . . this day we pause,
We, the miners of the iron-range, raise our ore-stained
      arms in farewell,
We, your friends of the Arrowhead,
Of the high hills of the Lake Superior wilds,
Of the Red River Valley,
Of the vast corn belt.

We are the men and women who till the soil, who man
      the machines,
Who rock the cradles, who perform the lowly tasks and
      the skilled tasks, so life may go on.

Yes, we pause in farewell, but also in gratitude
For while the trumpets of war blared,
While the world tumbled in chaos,
While the minds of men were trapped in fear,
There stood in the midst of the global circus

A brave, good woman, who spoke calmly, who spoke
   with the voice of sanity.

And her mother heart was great enough to fold within
   its embrace
All humanity, the children of all lands, all races, all
   creeds.

Dear friend, we are mindful today of your great labor
      in helping to build the road that leads to peace
      . . . to freedom . . . to justice.
We are mindful of the wisdom which widened the road
      so many could pass;
We are mindful of the stardust you sprinkled on the
      path, the stardust of your eloquence which kindled
      the way with hope and desire.

For all these, lovely friend, we shall remember you.
For all these, cherished friend, we have loved you.
For all these, courageous friend, we salute your memory.

Greetings were read from Judge Totten and Elmer Benson.
Oscar Christianson, Norwegian farmer, spoke from the floor.
   "I can say the greatest tribute to Marian and Arthur Le
Sueur is the tribute the farmers could pay them. As a pioneer
of Gray County I was always deeply impressed with their great
service to our cause."

The next speaker was Susie Stageberg, from the old days
of the speaker in the field, the parade of Farmer-Laborites at
Red Wing with yellow paint thrown on their cars. She was
a strong mother and fighter, the same age as Marian Le Sueur,

the wife of a scholar, a Christian Socialist, a woman difficult to break, who now lives alone on a hill above the Mississippi writing a book on the Farmer-Labor Party.

"When she fell she left 'a lonesome place against the sky.' Instead of mourning let us look up and address her in the words of the poet; 'Thy day has come, not gone; the sun has risen, not set; Thy life is now beyond the reach of death or change. Not ended, but begun, O noble soul, O gentle heart. Hail but not farewell.'

"And so too we would hail the imperishable spirit of our beloved Marian Le Sueur."

James Robertson, Chairman of the Progressive Party, spoke:

"It was in 1917 I first met Marian and through the years she has been constantly fighting on the side of the common people. In 1952 in a year of danger, at the age of seventy-five, she became the Progressive Party candidate for U.S. Senator, she organized, wrote, worked, she said she wanted to put the last lick in for the people.

"She did not win the election, of course, but she won the respect of every person in the country.

"Over and over she said I have faith in the people.

"Our people will build a greater, freer and more beautiful America, that was her wish, her vision. We must make that vision a reality."

Ralph Ahlstrom spoke of her "trial" as a "Red" before the State Legislature when she was appointed to the Board of Education.

"She will have a place in history. History has an ironic way with it. The real people will be read about in years to come and the witch hunters forgotten."

Walfred Engdahl spoke for the Social Science Study Club:

"She was a dreamer whose dreams are founded upon the actualities of life. She dreamed that the peoples of the world would become one all-embracing family. She dreamed of a time when there would be no masters and no slaves.

"She did not fail us in her dreams and inexhaustible efforts."

She was one of the first presidents of the Farmer-Labor Women's Club and so there were women who had known her many years. Mrs. Carlson of the Women's Progressive Party Club spoke, her voice shaking a little and then coming out full:

"She was a wondrous woman. She was a leader and inspiration to all womankind, championing every just cause and battling with them, against all the inequities and injustices."

And Mrs. Hawkins spoke for the Saturday Lunch Club:

"We can achieve what they dreamed, the land of the free and the home of the brave but only the brave can be free. The nation is renewed from the bottom and not from the top. It comes like the natural growth of a great tree, that genius springs up from the ranks of unknown men and women renewing the youth and energy of the people. The great, struggling, unknown mass at the base is the force which lifts the level of society. Our nation is as great and only as great as our rank and file."

Meridel Le Sueur stepped beside her daughter and the granddaughter of Marian Le Sueur and together they read the poem written for her by Irene Paull; the faces now were broken to love and weeping . . . leaning forward to catch not only

82

the words but to harvest the feeling and store in ferment for future courage.

> "Lay a flower upon her sleeping hair, my daughter,
> For you have thanks to give her before you say farewell.
> Do you walk with an air of easy freedom?
> Then give her thanks
> For it is she who hacked your freedom out of rock.
> Do you walk as an equal at your husband's side?
> Then remember her well
> Who hurled defiance at her husband's scorn
> And with her little children in her arms, slashed new
>   paths for you to travel
> Derision beating like hail upon her face.

> And you, my son, give thanks that you shall know because
>   of her
> A comradeship our fathers never knew
> Because no man is comrade to a slave.

> She was no smiling Madonna
> The sweet and self-effacing portrait of a woman,
> Painted so many centuries by countless men
> She was fierce as a bird is fierce that has to fly over high
>   and lonely crags,
> With angry claws she tore at prejudice and scorn
> And swooped like a hawk on all who'd rob her children
>   of their new won heights.

> Lay a flower upon her sleeping hair, my daughter,
> For all her heartache and her lonely pain,
> For all her sweetness hammered to pointed steel

To better battle for your womanhood and mine.

Lay a flower upon her sleeping hair and cherish her
As you cherish the sea
And mountains that climb the sky."

AFTERWORD

This book has always been special to me. I have read and re-read it all of my life—I can't even remember the first reading. Arthur (whom I called Bampa) died when I was two and Marian (Granny) when I was five, but they have been with me all of my life: this small book has served as a meeting place in which I continue to talk to them, listen to them, and learn from our history.

Crusaders is history, but it is unlike most history books. This book makes no mention of kings and generals, how wars were started and who won them. Instead it is about the women and men who built, settled, and peopled this country.

While this book is about Arthur and Marian Le Sueur, two heroes of the Midwest, it is more than that. It is the story of the thousands and thousands of women and men who formed labor, farmers', and political organizations, and who organized each other to build democracy in this young country. We do not know most of their names, but every day we reap the harvest of their commitment. Every time we go to a public library, every time someone who is not a rich, white, landowning male casts a ballot, every time a rural resident switches on a light, every time an urban dweller walks through one of our parks, every time our unions fight to save or improve our jobs, we are enjoying a benefit, a benefit that was hard-won from the powers of money and greed.

We reap the harvest they have sown in a more literal sense also, for we are their children, grandchildren, great-grandchildren, and great-great-grandchildren. The sad truth is that most of us don't know it. The children of the 240,000 members of the Non-Partisan League, the grandchildren of the million people who voted for Debs, are here today, but our ancestors have been stolen from us. The publishers of the textbooks, the owners of the broadcast media, have chosen our history and our heroes for us. In our collective enforced amnesia we are without the roots that give us hope and history.

Meridel, my grandmother, has given me a great gift. I have known my great-grandparents and through them I have learned about living a life. In these pages I heard discussions about principles, about not selling out, and about having something to stand for. Marian and Arthur believed in democracy. They believed that each citizen had a duty to participate, and that only with an educated, activist public could democracy work. When Arthur wrote his long letters to each new president, telling what he thought the president should do, he was not naive enough to think that he would always be listened to, but he believed that he was doing what he had to do. I have always been able to ask myself, "What would Marian and Arthur have done in this situation?" and although it has been thirty years since I have talked to them, from within myself I find an answer. I cannot overestimate the worth of this book to my life.

Now the Minnesota Historical Society is giving more of us this same gift by reprinting this volume. Marian and Arthur are also your grandparents—Meridel chose to share them when she wrote this book. We all hope that their story gives all of you strength, hope, and commitment to end this century the way the Crusaders started it.

David Tilsen
Great-grandson of
Arthur and Marian Le Sueur

Antoinette Lucy

Marian Wharton with Meridel and Winston, 1906

Marian Wharton, 1908

Arthur Le Sueur

ART. LeSUEUR

The Great Socialist
and Labor Champion
Will Address
THE FIRST SOCIALIST CONVENTION
Held in Benson County at Baker, N. D.
FRIDAY MARCH, 13, 1914
2 O'CLOCK P. M.

Poster, 1914

A
Message
TO THE
Men
AND
Women
OF
America

THREE DAY COURSE

BY

MARIAN WHARTON

ON

THE GREAT LAWS OF LIFE

Pamphlet advertising lectures, 1913

Antoinette Lucy taking leave of Marian and Arthur Le Sueur, Fort Scott, Kansas, 1917. Antoinette stayed behind as the Le Sueurs fled to St. Paul.

Marian and Arthur Le Sueur, about 1917

Meridel Le Sueur, about 1911

Meridel Le Sueur with her daughter Rachel, 1931

Meridel Le Sueur, 1981. PHOTOGRAPH BY JEROME LIEBLING

GLOSSARY

SUSAN B. ANTHONY, 1820-1906, leader in the struggles for women's rights, emancipation of the Negro people, and their full equality with whites.

BERGER, VICTOR, 1860-1929, first Socialist Congressman in U.S., elected from Wisconsin.

BERKMAN, ALEXANDER, 1870-1936, an American anarchist and associate of Emma Goldman.

BLOOMER, AMELIA, 1818-1894, leader in the struggle for women's rights, including revision of marriage laws, suffrage, the right to independent work, and dress reform.

CHARTISM. A powerful political movement of British workers. In 1838 leaders of the London Working Men's Association drew up "the People's Charter," demanding universal manhood suffrage, annual parliaments, vote by ballot, abolition of property qualifications for House membership, payment of Members of Parliament and equal electoral districts.

CHRISTIAN SOCIALISM. A doctrine originating in England but spreading to other countries, which attempted to combine the religious teachings of Christianity with the theories of Socialism.

DE LEON, DANIEL, 1852-1914. Leader of the Socialist Labor Party; one of the founders of the I.W.W.; advocate of industrial unionism.

DONNELLY, IGNATIUS, 1831-1901. Member of Republican Party in pre-Civil War period; member of Congress from Minnesota. Later supporter of the Granger and Greenback movements, and still later a leader of the Farmers' Alliance and the Populist Party.

FARMERS' ALLIANCE. The name is applied to two organizations, the National Farmers' Alliance in the Northwest, and the National Farmers' Alliance and Industrial Union in the

South. They were active in the 1870's, 1880's, and 1890's to curb monopoly practices harmful to middle and smaller farmers.

GOLDMAN, EMMA, 1869-1940. An American of anarchist views.

THE GRANGE. An organization of farmers begun in 1867 to fight monopoly practices of railroads and elevators, and to buy and sell co-operatively.

HILLQUIT, MORRIS, 1869-1933, a leader of the Socialist Party in the U.S.

HAYWOOD, WILLIAM D., 1869-1928. Advocate of industrial unionism; secretary-treasurer of the Western Federation of Miners; one of the founders and leaders of the I.W.W.; Socialist.

I.W.W. Industrial Workers of the World, an organization of unions begun in 1905. Unlike the American Federation of Labor, it was organized along industrial, not craft, lines, and followed a policy of syndicalism.

INGERSOLL, ROBERT G., 1833-1899, American attorney and agnostic famous as an anti-religious lecturer.

KEY, ELLEN, 1849-1926, Swedish worker in the cause of women's rights, including suffrage; also an advocate of sex education.

KIRKPATRICK, GEORGE, leading U.S. Socialist and candidate for Vice-President on the Socialist Party ticket in 1916.

KNIGHTS OF LABOR, a broad organization of labor founded in 1869.

LAFOLLETTE, ROBERT M., 1855-1925. Governor of Wisconsin, U.S. Senator, opponent of imperialism and imperialist war, and independent third-party candidate for President in 1924.

MOTT, LUCRETIA, 1793-1880, a leader in the causes of Abolition of slavery and of women's rights; also a station agent on the underground railroad.

NATION, CARRIE, 1846-1911, temperance agitator.

NATIONAL NON-PARTISAN LEAGUE, an organization begun in 1915 by wheat farmers rebelling against monopoly practices in the grain trade.

PINKERTONS. The Pinkerton Detective Agency, founded in 1850, soon made spying upon labor organizations its main task.

POPULISTS. A common name for the People's Party, formed in 1892. It grew chiefly out of the political activities of the Farmers Alliances and other farm organizations, and was supported by the Knights of Labor and various unions.

RED SPECIAL. The train in which Eugene Victor Debs, candidate of the Socialist Party, made a country-wide tour in 1908.

REMITTANCE MEN. Under the British feudal land laws, younger sons could not inherit land. Many of them went out to colonies and were granted a monthly remittance by their families.

RUSSELL, CHARLES EDWARD, 1860-1921, progressive journalist and Socialist Party worker.

RUTHENBERG, CHARLES EMIL, 1882-1927, first secretary of the Communist Party of the United States.

SHAW, ANNA HOWARD, 1847-1919, physician, ordained Methodist preacher and fighter for the rights of women.

SPARGO, JOHN, 1876-1966, Socialist editor and leader.

STANTON, ELIZABETH CADY, 1815-1902, a leader in the struggles for abolition of slavery and for woman suffrage, organizer of the 1848 Seneca Falls Convention which formally launched the woman's rights movement in the U.S.

STEINMETZ, CHARLES P., 1865-1923, famed mathematician, electrical engineer, and Socialist.

STONE, LUCY, 1818-1893, leader in the movements for the Abolition of slavery and for woman's rights.

SUGARED OFF. It was the practice of big companies to buy an acre of land, enough to set up a camp, and then to steal all the surrounding timber. This was "pure sugar" for the companies and was known as "sugaring off."

SYNDICALISM. A form of trade unionism, developed first in France, which opposes political action, calls for militant unionism and ascribes to the union the primary and leading role in changing society.

TOWNLEY, A. P., organizer for the Socialist Party, founder of the Non-Partisan League.

WAGENKNECHT, ALFRED, 1881-1956, a leader of the Socialist and later of the Communist Party.

WARREN, FRED, an editor of the *Appeal to Reason.*

WILLARD, FRANCES, 1839-1898, a leader in the movement for woman suffrage and for temperance.

WOLLSTONECRAFT, MARY, 1759-1797. British fighter for women's liberation, author of the epoch-making book "A Vindication of the Rights of Woman" (1792).

WORK, JOHN M., a leader of the Socialist Party.

INDEX